MW01062184

LIVES OF GREAT RELIGIOUS BOOKS

The Passover Haggadah

LIVES OF GREAT RELIGIOUS BOOKS

The Passover Haggadah, Vanessa L. Ochs
Josephus's *The Jewish War,* Martin Goodman
The *Song of Songs,* Ilana Pardes
The Life of Saint Teresa of Avila, Carlos Eire
The Book of *Exodus,* Joel S. Baden
The Book of *Revelation,* Timothy Beal
The *Talmud,* Barry Scott Wimpfheimer
The *Koran* in English, Bruce B. Lawrence
The *Lotus Sūtra,* Donald S. Lopez, Jr.
John Calvin's *Institutes of the Christian Religion,* Bruce Gordon
C. S. Lewis's *Mere Christianity,* George M. Marsden
The *Bhagavad Gita,* Richard H. Davis
The *Yoga Sutra of Patanjali,* David Gordon White
Thomas Aquinas's *Summa theologiae,* Bernard McGinn
The *Book of Common Prayer,* Alan Jacobs
The Book of *Job,* Mark Larrimore
The *Dead Sea Scrolls,* John J. Collins
The Book of *Genesis,* Ronald Hendel
The *Book of Mormon,* Paul C. Gutjahr
The *I Ching,* Richard J. Smith
The Tibetan Book of the Dead, Donald S. Lopez, Jr.
Augustine's *Confessions,* Garry Wills
Dietrich Bonhoeffer's *Letters and Papers from Prison,* Martin E. Marty

The Passover Haggadah

A BIOGRAPHY

Vanessa L. Ochs

PRINCETON UNIVERSITY PRESS

Princeton and Oxford

Published by Princeton University Press
41 William Street, Princeton, New Jersey 08540
6 Oxford Street, Woodstock, Oxfordshire OX20 1TR

press.princeton.edu

Library of Congress Cataloging-in-Publication Data
Names: Ochs, Vanessa L., author.
Title: The Passover Haggadah : a biography / Vanessa Ochs.
Other titles: Lives of great religious books. Description: Princeton,
    New Jersey : Princeton University Press, 2020. | Series: Lives of great
    religious books | Includes bibliographical references and index.
Identifiers: LCCN 2019030565 (print) | LCCN 2019030566 (ebook)
    | ISBN 9780691144986 (hardcover) | ISBN 9780691201528 (epub)
Subjects: LCSH: Haggadah—History. | Haggadot—Texts—History and
    criticism.
Classification: LCC BM674.79 .O33 2020 (print) | LCC BM674.79
    (ebook) | DDC 296.4/5371—dc23
LC record available at https://lccn.loc.gov/2019030565
LC ebook record available at https://lccn.loc.gov/2019030566

British Library Cataloging-in-Publication Data is available

Editorial: Fred Appel and Jenny Tan
Production Editorial: Debbie Tegarden
Production: Erin Suydam
Publicity: Kathryn Stevens
Copyeditor: Dawn Hall

Jacket image: Barbara Wolff, "Ma Nishtanah," from the *Rose Haggadah*, 2014.
Collection of The Morgan Library and Museum, New York (MS.M. 1191).

This book has been composed in Garamond Premier Pro

Printed on acid-free paper. ∞

Printed in the United States of America

10 9 8 7 6 5 4 3 2 1

For Harry, Emma, and Isaiah

CONTENTS

LIST OF ILLUSTRATIONS   ix

INTRODUCTION: The Life of the Haggadah   1

CHAPTER 1   How the Haggadah Came to Be:
             Early Sources in the Bible, Tosefta,
             Mishnah, Talmud, and Midrash   18

CHAPTER 2   On Becoming a Book: From the
             Earliest Haggadot to the Illuminated
             Haggadot of the Middle Ages   40

CHAPTER 3   The Printed Haggadah and Its
             Enduring Conventions: A Text
             of One's Own   67

CHAPTER 4   Twentieth-Century Variations:
             The Haggadah in American Jewish
             Movements, Israeli Kibbutzim,
             and American Third Seders   90

CHAPTER 5   Haggadot of Darkness   113

CHAPTER 6   The Haggadah of the Moment   139

ACKNOWLEDGMENTS   175

RESOURCES   177

GLOSSARY   179

NOTES   181

INDEX   197

LIST OF ILLUSTRATIONS

FIGURE 2.1   Birds' Head Haggadah, The Israel Museum,
             Jerusalem, Photo © Israel Museum, Jerusalem,
             by Ardon Bar Hama Digital photography
             funded by George S. Blumenthal, New
             York.   51

FIGURE 2.2   Washington Haggadah, Elijah and others
             on donkey, Stern, *Washington Haggadah*,
             f. 19v.   63

FIGURE 3.1   Amsterdam Haggadah, 1695, Four Sons.   77

FIGURE 3.2   Second Cincinnati Haggadah, 1716–1717,
             Four Sons, produced by Mosheh Leib ben
             Volf, Trebitsch, Moravia, Ms. 444 First
             Cincinnati Haggadah, Klau Library,
             Cincinnati, Hebrew Union College–Jewish
             Institute of Religion.   78

FIGURE 3.3   Amsterdam Haggadah, 1695, frontispiece:
             Aaron and Moses.   80

FIGURE 3.4   King James Bible, 1611, frontispiece: Aaron
             and Moses.   81

FIGURE 5.1   Offenbacher Haggadah, Israelites crossing the
             sea, Pharaoh's army drowns, courtesy of the
             Leo Baeck Institute.   115

FIGURE 5.2   The Szyk Haggadah, 1935, The Bread of
             Affliction. Reproduced with cooperation
             of Irvin Ungar.   120
FIGURE 6.1   A seder plate with coconut, an orange, sticks
             and stones, flowers, pickled vegetables, and
             fruit salad. Photo credited to Asher Gellis,
             creator of the LGBTQ Seder Plate. First
             fully integrated LGBTQ and Ally Haggadah
             created and available at https://www
             .haggadot.com/haggadah/jq-international
             -glbt-haggadah.   157

The Passover Haggadah

The Life of the Haggadah

When I began to think hard about the life of the Haggadah in preparation for this biography, Rabbi Lawrence Hoffman, who has written extensively on this text, suggested I go to Chicago and meet Stephen Durchslag, the premier private collector of the printed Haggadah in America. I'm glad I did, because shortly after my arrival, I learned how the Haggadah lived in a distinctive way.

The father of anthropological fieldwork is Bronislaw Malinowski, who distinguished himself from the armchair anthropologists of the nineteenth century by leaving home and going into the field for an extended period to live among the people who would be the objects of his study; in those days, they were invariably called "the natives." Malinowski's description of his arrival in Melanesian New Guinea is well known. "Imagine yourself," Malinowski wrote, "suddenly set down surrounded by all your gear, alone on a tropical beach close to a native village, while the launch or dinghy which has brought you sails away, out of sight."[1] The entrance story foreshadows the anthropologist's transformation from stranger to insider. It also hints at essential understandings that will be revealed. While anthropologists today rarely

claim they have become insiders, performing fieldwork remains their primary research method and is the profession's
initiation rite. They still tell entrance stories, so, nodding to
Malinowski, I preface this biography with my own.

I arrived along the shore of Lake Michigan, neither by
launch nor by dinghy, but by car. This was Chicago's Gold
Coast, and I stood in front of the grand building where
Mr. Durchslag, who had invited me to call him Steve, lived,
hoping I was presentable. It was an unusually sunny and
hot fall day. When I entered his modern, art-filled apart-
ment overlooking the city and the lake, he graciously offered me a drink. I said, "Water will be lovely." I felt awe
and excitement as Steve ushered me into his wood-shelved
library where his Haggadot were housed. (In Hebrew, the
plural of Haggadah is Haggadot; still, many people say
"Haggadahs," an Anglicized mash-up of the Yiddish plural,
hagodes.) Rare ones were just there on the shelves, not even
behind glass, but placed along with his other books, even
paperbacks. He selected treasures to show me, rapidly placing one on top of the next on a glass display table in the
center of the room. Here was the 1629 Venice Haggadah,
the 1695 Amsterdam Haggadah, and now the 1712 Amsterdam with its fold-out map of the biblical world. I could
hardly keep up. Steve didn't insist I coddle each Haggadah
on a special foam rest as I had in libraries' rare books collections; this was liberating, but what if I stressed the binding? He didn't ask me to put on those special white gloves
the special collections librarians made me wear. I could
have been perusing my very modest shelf of stacked up
Haggadot in my living room, a "collection" rich in the
supermarket and Maxwell House coffee Haggadot my

mother had amassed over years, not as exemplars of ephemera, but for us to use. I was anxious for the safety of Steve's books—didn't they need a more watchful eye, some protection, say, from me?

Distracting myself from these worrisome thoughts, I asked Steve how he had found his Haggadot, thinking he might have some miraculous discovery stories. He answered by matter-of-factly pulling off a Sotheby's catalog and then one from Kestenbaum's from his shelves; he pointed to a new purchase that was still in an unopened padded mailer, and he said more new ones were on their way. The tower of Haggadot he was piling on the table for me grew higher. Haggadot from Poona (Pune), Paris, South Africa, Shanghai, Melbourne, Munich. He declared it was time to clear off this batch to make space for others.

Inebriated by gratitude to be present to witness this wondrous collection, I enthusiastically stretched out my right arm over the books on the table, ready to help sweep them up so I could see even more rare Haggadot.

I had failed to notice that on this hot day, Steve had also gotten himself a drink, a bottle of diet cola, and it had been on the table all along, and it was uncapped. Now, thanks to my outstretched arm, it was spilling all over the table of Haggadot. I prayed: "Oh dear God, if the soda damages just the Sotheby's catalog—that would be enough. Or just the Sotheby's and also, the Kestenbaum's; even that would be enough."

I started to turn toward Steve, anticipating his horror and displaying my shame, but during my liturgical interlude, he had dashed off and returned with what he called a *shmatta*, a little towel. He was already clearing, dabbing, mopping, and reassuring me: "You cannot treat them as artifacts, or they lose their value."

That is when I understood that while an individual Haggadah may be collected and cherished for its historical or artistic merits, it lives as its most authentic self when it is used, especially on a family's Passover seder table. That is when it "gets a life," so to speak. In that place of vulnerability, subject to wine spills and the assault of matzah crumbs, it choreographs the transmission of particular memories and inculcates sensibilities. I would go on to learn that a Haggadah comes to life when it leads those who have gathered to use it to ask hard questions about slavery, exile, redemption, and freeing the oppressed. Its liveliness increases each time it is taken out again to be used at a seder and each time celebrants use it. It is especially lively, but in a different way, when it fades into the background and gives rise to the conversation of those seated at the seder table, who are alive at the present moment and make telling the Passover story meaningful for themselves.

Writer James Salter introduced his memoir, *Burning the Days: Recollection*, as "more or less the story of a life. Not the complete story which, as in almost any case, is beyond telling—the length would be too great, longer than Proust, not to speak of the repetition." This biography of the Haggadah is also more or less the story of a life. The word Haggadah means "telling" and the complete story of its life—spanning more than six thousand versions over millennia—would be beyond telling and unspeakably repetitive. Just as Salter selected from the parts of his life that were important to him, a different biographer of the Haggadah—say, a scholar of rabbinic literature, a historian of the Jewish book, or an expert in

Jewish illuminated manuscripts—would make choices and craft a telling based on his or her frame of reference within the highly specialized (and brutally competitive, I have observed) academic field of Haggadah study. As the author of this telling, I recollect the life of the Haggadah by selecting versions and aspects that have engaged me and stimulated my speculation. What you have before you is not encyclopedic. It is personal, partial, and eclectic, and it reflects my being an anthropologist who investigates Jewish ritual innovation in the contemporary era. This means that when I turn backward, I do so unabashedly from a twenty-first-century perspective.

I will be introducing many versions of the Haggadah, including ones often reproduced, those deemed important for their rarity and beauty or their introduction of new artistic conventions and book-making technologies. We will also encounter versions that reflect the range of Jewish geographic distribution; disclose variations in Jewish practice; register historically significant events; or address liturgical, pedagogical, and theological matters. Making selections has been a challenge, for just about any Haggadah is a worthy springboard for reflection. Even the free supermarket Haggadah (with coupons for matzah and horseradish in the centerfold pages—I kid you not!) reflects an important facet of its story.

What Is the Haggadah?

This telling of the life of the Haggadah chronicles its recalibrations over time. We will move from its early sources in the Bible and rabbinic literature; to the years it was a handwritten manuscript; to its life as an illuminated book in the middle ages; to its emergence as a mass-produced printed book and later, as an artist's book; to its iterations in the twentieth century in America and Israel, including those that reflect the Holocaust; and finally to the current explosion of new versions, including those using emerging technologies of our day.

Let us begin with a broad-stroked overview.

The Haggadah's life as a liturgical text came about to fulfill a biblical injunction to fathers to tell the story of the Exodus from Egypt to their children (literally, to their sons): "And you shall tell your son on that day, 'It is because of what the Lord did for me when I went free from Egypt'" (Exodus 13:8). For those Jewish men who lacked children, their students could fill in; for the childless without students, wives would do. Persons all alone could still tell the story to themselves, asking the questions and answering them, too. Transmit that memory of holy history as if it happened to you, as if you were there yourself among the children of Israel. Its essence: we were slaves, God rescued us once from degradation and brought us to freedom as a nation, and we are as grateful now as we were then. The moral: cherish freedom, or, lacking it, seek it out. And trust: the next redemption, however bleak the current moment, may be just around the bend. Transmit that memory of oppression captivatingly enough so the story attaches itself to the moral imagination. The memory of belonging to a people who knew slavery and then liberation should enliven so much empathy that one cannot help but feel responsible for helping others to achieve their own liberation.

In the biblical story of the children of Israel wandering in the desert, they are exhorted to explain to their children why they sacrificed lambs in the spring. While the First and Second Temples in Jerusalem stood, during Passover pilgrimages, the sacrifices took place in their vicinity. Following the destruction of the Second Temple (70 CE), and some say, even before that, the sacrifice was made symbolically with food and drink and an interpretive liturgy, including narration, and it took place in homes.

From the beginning of the diaspora from the Land of Israel until this day, the obligation of transmission is still carried out in the form of a step-by-step dining practice called the *seder*. The word means order. It refers to the order in which one recites the Passover liturgy, drinks four cups of wine, and engages ritually with symbolic foods by breaking, dipping, indicating, or hiding and seeking them. The seder is part Greco-Roman symposium (to be discussed later), part study and prayer session, part holiday dinner at Grandma and Grandpa's house, and with growing frequency, part teach-in for social justice or political protest. Because a spirit of rejoicing on Passover (one of the three Jewish pilgrimage festivals; the others are Sukkot in the fall and Shavuot in late spring) is called for, the seder table became the site for a festive repast. There, under the spell of narrative and ritual, all the other degradations, exiles, and cries of the past might be briefly repressed; all enemies, past and future, are imagined as getting their due. In a passage expressing the horror of being slaughtered by Crusader armies in 1096, there is a cry for vengeance, one that has been a source of discomfort for some who adamantly omit it on the grounds of xenophobia: "Pour out Your wrath on the nations that do not know You . . . ; annihilate them from under God's heavens."

What exactly can you find in a fairly traditional Haggadah? I offer this synopsis: The Haggadah begins with a list of the fourteen steps that characterize the proceedings. Next comes the first of four blessings over wine, and instructions for washing one's hands, saying a blessing over a green vegetable, and breaking a matzah and setting half aside for hiding. It is followed by a minisummary that explains why Passover is observed and introduces the theme of slavery and freedom. Next, a child asks four questions, which are only vaguely answered; there is a story of four archetypal children, the questions they ask, and the answers they receive. Many passages of rabbinic literature that elliptically refer to the Exodus are eventually enlivened by instructions to name the ten plagues as well as by a cheerful song called "Dayenu" (it would be enough), which expresses gratitude for all of God's graciousness to the children of Israel along their journey. Psalms follow, and then comes a burst of ritual action: handwashing, a blessing before eating matzah, another one for eating bitter herbs, and a ritual for eating a sandwich made of the bitter herbs and a condiment called *charoset*. Finally, it is time for a festive meal. This is followed by instructions to eat the retrieved matzah half, a grace after meals, a welcome to the prophet Elijah, then more psalms, a statement of completion, and a selection of popular liturgical songs that have accrued over the years.

The Haggadah has no single author and no single editor. From the time of "tell your child," spanning oral to written cultures, the Haggadah has grown into a commonplace book chronicling generations of verbal, illustrative, and ritual strategies that were considered, in their times and in their places, suitable for the task of transmission. Recite this! Teach that! Imbibe and ingest the sweet fruit and nut paste called charoset, the bitter herbs, the springy greens, the flat-crunchy matzah! Remember worse times, pray for better ones! Told with bursts of eloquence, courtesy of the psalms recited before and after the meal, and climaxing in loveable cumulative ditties, the assemblage of direction, prayer, and teaching became codified along the way. It has made for a night of dinner theater, in which cast and audience are one and the same as they utter, "It is because of what the Lord did for me when I went forth from Egypt" (Exodus 13:8). From the very start, qualities such as deep empathy, flexibility, fluidity, and personalization were attached to this practice of oral transmission performed communally and intergenerationally. If the gambit worked, heritage and obligation would be transmitted. The newest generation would know what their parents had known: how to remember their way into tribal belonging. Come the next year, the initiation would be repeated with age-appropriate nods to children's growing skills, attention spans, and possible alienation, and thus, membership and the experience of belonging would be intensified.

While the Haggadah shapes the way the Exodus narrative is told, how the sacramental foods are eaten, and how God is to be acknowledged, there is—now especially—significant range in how much authority a Haggadah asserts. On one extreme, there are those who follow their texts to the letter; they can even find, in the small print, instructions for how to measure the precise amounts of matzah that must be eaten. On the other extreme, there are many, worldwide, who skip over what seems just too much. They include the father of playwright Tony Kushner, whose skipping practices are humorously recalled in his 1995 play "Notes on Akiba" written for a third seder performance piece at the Jewish Museum in New York. (Here's why his father skips the section about the ten plagues: it is "lengthy, too close to dinner to be endured, and exceedingly blood-curdling."[2])

Recently, a blogger from Hawaii found her childhood Haggadot while cleaning out her mother's basement in Kansas City and wrote:

> My father's copy is carefully marked in red pen so he could lead our seder . . . to dinner as efficiently as possible. He even wrote the word "Skip" in many places. Thank goodness. The Gershun family has always been short on seder and long on food! We definitely follow that tradition in this Gershun home to this day.[3]

Some quit their seders midway, putting aside their Haggadot for good when the festive meal is served. While some use an abridged version (even a Passover coloring book, even after the children are now grown!) and are done in minutes, others, proud that their seders extend into the wee hours, make it to the very last pages. Their Haggadah might inspire interruptions: debates, classical teachings that come to mind, new readings, specially composed songs and dances, and planned and spontaneous dramatizations. I think of the Passover my mother, who had just received a walking stick and a cape for her April birthday, took up on the spur of the moment and called herself Grandma Moses. She led a mid-seder parade of little grandchildren rushing through the living room until they were chased by Pharaoh's invisible army as they crossed the laundry room, which she designated as the "sea." A few years back, in an unscripted portion of the seder, my colleague, a Jewish Studies professor, put his Haggadah down and invited his preschoolers to break, piñata-style, the gold-painted modern-day idol he had constructed for them out of cardboard: a larger-than-life computer. Such instances of home-style performance art may evoke 1960s happenings, but they are actually inspired by even earlier generations of Jews who have been lively Haggadah enactors.

The Haggadah is unlike most other Jewish texts in terms of the laws that govern its usage. Let me explain. Whereas Jewish law stipulates that the Torah scroll must be read from and the Scroll of Esther must be heard, no laws stipulate how the Haggadah should be read aloud or heard. While there is usually a leader who chants the Haggadah or directs those around the table to take parts, one could read it quietly to oneself and perform the required ritual acts. As with the Torah, there are traditions of cantillation for singing the Haggadah that have been passed down in Judaism's different ethnic groups, but this is a home ceremony, so no guardians stand by to correct words that are inadvertently skipped or misread.

Conceivably, given that the Haggadah is constructed as a script or prompt, one could not use a Haggadah at all and conduct a Passover seder from memory. Until codified, Jewish liturgy, law, and learning were orally transmitted; the grand exception was the written Torah scroll. Orality preserved the dynamism of Jewish tradition, its freshness. If a memorized general script for the seder might have once been sufficient for a people with a strong oral tradition, it eventually ceased being so, except in moments of terrible trials, such as during the Holocaust, when for some, the only available Haggadah was the Haggadah of memory.

The Haggadah also has a distinctive life as a Jewish ritual object. Containing the name of God, protocols of respect must be observed. Drop it and it is kissed. When it is worn out, it should be stored in a repository called a *geniza* until it can be buried. Such considerations aside, the Haggadah is considered less sacred than a Torah scroll. (The rule of thumb: the more sacred an object is considered, the more rules there are governing its production and usage.) A Torah must be handwritten on sheets of parchment made from the skin of a kosher animal (usually from a cow) that has been soaked in limewater, stretched, and scraped. The ink is made of plant gall, copper sulfate crystals, gum arabic, and water and is applied with a quill from a kosher goose or a turkey. It is written out precisely and accurately using traditional letterings, spacing, and columns. No illustrations. The sheets of parchment are sewn together with strings of animal sinew and wound on wooden rollers. If there is an error in the Torah scroll or any defacement, it is not kosher, fit for use, the same word used to describe foods permitted to a Jew. This work can only be done by a ritual scribe, called a *sofer*, who prepares for the day's work with prayer and ablution.

While there are some more or less established conventions for a Haggadah's layout, there is no protocol for how it must be written. What inks, paints, or paper can be used? How should it be bound? It's up for grabs.

There is no protocol for storage and handling. The Torah scroll, crowned with a silver headpiece or silk scarves and wrapped in embroidered velvet or enclosed upright in a decorated metal or wooden box, is taken from an often ornate ark that is the focal point of the synagogue's architecture. Before and after it is read from, it is processed before congregants who have risen in its honor and reach out to transfer a kiss on it by hand, prayer book, or fringe of the prayer shawl. The choreography makes it clear: the Torah represents both God's word and God's palpable presence. There is no elaborate choreography for Haggadot, kept mostly at home. True, they may get places of honor on bookshelves next to other Jewish texts. An especially lovely Haggadah may be displayed and given pride of place in the living room alongside a Hanukkah candelabra, which, together with a mezuzah on the door, indicate a Jewish American home. (Interestingly enough, many Jews who have Haggadot at home won't have a Bible or prayer book.) Likely enough, after Passover, most Haggadot are stacked in batches, rubber-banded, packed away in a box along with the Passover dishes and the chopping bowl, and stored in the basement, attic, or closet until they get taken out again next year. Come Passover eve, like spring crocuses, they appear again, perhaps a little worse for wear. But who notices? It's a sometimes scruffy, familiar item.

Rare Haggadot have been stored in mundane places, though not necessarily on purpose. In 2013, an auctioneer appraising the contents of a home in North Manchester, England, discovered an ornately illustrated eighteenth-century Haggadah made by a scribe to the imperial court in Vienna for the Oppenheim banking family. It was languishing in an Osem soup carton in the garage! It had apparently come from Belgium to Britain when its owners escaped the Nazis, but the current owners had no idea they even owned it, let alone how it had come into the family's possession. Dr. Yaakov Wise of the Centre for Jewish Studies at the University of Manchester said of this miraculous discovery: "This was probably in use for 200 years. There are wine and food stains on it which is exactly what you would expect when it was at the table. It is easy to imagine the wealthy family in Vienna sitting around in their wigs and their buckled shoes reading it by candlelight."[4] It was later sold at auction for $340,000.

A Haggadah has a life as an object that is viewed, but not used, in museum and library collections, and they are found in private Judaica collections as well. Everyday people collect Haggadot too, sometimes purposefully—say, by purchasing a new one each year—and often by chance—it's quite easy to walk out of a supermarket with a free (or "free with a purchase") copy. OK, I confess: a few free copies.

There have been exquisite Haggadot, including illuminated versions of the medieval period, publications in the new age of printing, and periodic revivals of illumination, including the arresting mid-twentieth-century Haggadah of Arthur Syzk. In our age, there have been fine art versions, originals, limited editions, and mass-produced copies. Some of my personal favorite Haggadah artists are Zoya Cherkassy, Maty Grünberg, Tamar Messer, Avner Moriah, Mark Podwal, Ben Shahn, Eliyahu Sidi, and Barbara Wolff.

An exceptional Haggadah designated as a collector's item generates veneration and might spend its days at the Jewish National Library in Jerusalem (which is said to have the world's largest collection of Haggadot—over 10,000!), the British Library, the Bodleian, the Library of Congress, the New York Public Library, the library of the Jewish Theological Seminary, the Morgan Library, and even the

Vatican—not to mention in university libraries, synagogues, Jewish museums, or private homes. Still, there is pride of place for a workaday variant, such as one that has been passed down by family members and distinguished by the patina of love and memory; its link to generations past stimulates a loving respect and attaches an extra freight of meaning.

How many versions of the Haggadah are there? Determining that has fueled a cottage industry of Haggadah bibliographies. In 1901 there was Shmuel Wiener's *A Bibliography of the Passover Haggadah* listing 909 publications; Abraham Yaari's *A Bibliography of the Passover Haggadah* (1960) lists 2,700, and later increased the number by 174.[5] In his magisterial 1975 book *Haggadah in History*, which chronicles five centuries of the Haggadah in print, from its appearance in liturgical compendia to its existence as a freestanding volume, Yosef Hayim Yerushalmi characterized the Haggadah as "the most popular and beloved of Hebrew books." He tipped his hat to bibliographers who cataloged over 3,500 editions coming to light, the most reprinted, widely translated, frequently illustrated, and widely issued volume wherever Jewish presses have flourished.[6] Yitzhak Yudlov then compiled a 1997 *Haggadah Thesaurus* accounting for 4,715 Haggadot since the beginning of printing until 1960. Now, whenever figures are cited, the number is usually 5,000 and counting. Nearly every article about the Haggadah notes its many revisions, with Edward Rothstein in the April 17, 2011, *New York Times* offering one of the most eloquent accounts:

Though only read once or twice a year, it has probably had more wine spilled on it than any other book ever published. Over the centuries, it has been paraphrased, abridged, translated, transliterated and transformed. It has been sung, chanted, illustrated and supplanted. And in 5,000 or so editions since the invention of the printing press.[7]

Why so many? Why has the Haggadah resisted being fixed once and for all? To answer this question, I traveled around America and to Israel consulting with Haggadah experts—Jewish museum curators, Judaica librarians, collectors, scholars, rabbis, and those who have created and published Haggadot of their own. I inevitably heard three answers.

The first is geography, because Jews have lived all over the world. Since the Haggadah may be recited in any language so it can be understood, it has been printed in Hebrew and translated into English, Yiddish, Judeo-Italian, Judeo-Spanish, French, Spanish, Russian, Polish, Chinese, Italian, Croatian, Danish, Czech, Finnish, Turkish, Swedish, Hungarian, Amharic . . . just to name a few. An 1874 Haggadah written in Hebrew and Marathi depicting the Bene Israel Jews of India is often used to make this point of the diversity of Jewish settlement. In this same vein, we hear about community Haggadot from the seventeenth and eighteenth centuries, written in Hebrew, Aramaic, Chinese, and Judeo-Persian that were used by Jews who had settled in the Chinese city of Kaifeng.

The second answer is diversity of Jewish practice. The Haggadah has accommodated the many ways Judaism has been practiced and reflects different liturgical rites. We see that easily in contemporary America, with Haggadot created for Reform, Conservative, Reconstructionist, Orthodox, Sephardic, Ultra-Orthodox, Hasidic, Renewal, Humanist, and secular Jews as well as for those describing themselves as nondenominational or postdenominational.

History is the third answer. The Haggadah has expanded to chronicle events—especially crises and cataclysms—that have become assimilated into the story Jews tell about themselves at the annual ritual of peoplehood. Consider the Haggadah written during the Holocaust that comes with nightmarish illustrations reflecting concentration or DP camps. Consider, too, the many Israeli or American Haggadot issued soon after the Six-Day War of 1967 with celebratory images of Israeli soldiers praying at the Western Wall or whimsical drawings of Jerusalem's Old City. As it happens, there are Haggadot, such as the Schechter Haggadah, which, in addition to providing the traditional materials for the seder also tell the history of Jews through pictures and commentary. Jacob Ari Labendz has called them historiographical Haggadot because they reveal how Jews in different places and eras saw themselves observing Passover and also engage the reader in self-reflexive embedding. Think of the Morton Salt girl who carries a container of salt with smaller picture of herself—into an imagined infinitum. "It is as if they ask their reader to *look upon himself as though he were a Jew of another era looking upon himself 'as though he went out of Egypt.'*"[8]

In the course of this biography, we will see precisely how geography, practice, and history have occasioned revision . . . and, in all likelihood, will continue to do so. As we come to know the life of the Haggadah more intimately and learn how it has functioned as an organism, we shall see how its capacity to maintain a core and still be an ever-flexible work in process, produced with the ever-changing needs of the current celebrants and their situations in mind, has been a key to its longevity.

How the Haggadah Came to Be

Early Sources in the Bible, Tosefta, Mishnah, Talmud, and Midrash

The Bible[1] provides the backstory for the life of the Haggadah. It is the source of the exodus narrative and provides the core language, imagery, and the Haggadah's raison d'être. It's worth remembering that biblical narratives ordaining or describing observances of Passover are not the same as historical, ethnographic, or archaeological evidence. We don't know if there ever were actual men and women who performed the Passover rituals the ancient Israelites were commanded to observe precisely as they were described—or at all. Were practices that were presented as being newly instituted by God indeed so very new or distinctive to the Israelites? Did Israelite leaders and parents succeed in transmitting the social and spiritual attitudes the Passover practices were intended to inculcate? We have hints, but not facts.

If we were to read the Hebrew Bible from cover to cover as a literary narrative,[2] we would see that the story of the exodus is foreshadowed before the Israelites were enslaved in Egypt under Pharaoh, before they called out to God for rescue and Moses cried, "Let my people go!" It begins in Genesis, with an ancestral dream: "As the sun was about to set, a deep sleep fell upon Abram" (15:12). Abraham (known as Abram before his encounter with God) sets forth on his sacred journey away from the home of his idol-keeping family toward a land promised by the one God who has spoken to him. God comes to him in a night vision, revealing a terrifying future for Abraham's descendants: "Know well that your offspring shall be strangers in a land not their own, and they shall be enslaved and oppressed for four hundred years" (Genesis 15:13). God tempers the awful news with consolation: "I will execute judgment on the nation they shall serve, and in the end they shall go free with great wealth" (Genesis 15:14). The entire story is summarized in Deuteronomy 26:10–14. Israel's sacred history, declared at harvest time, later becomes the core of the Haggadah's narrative.

Biblical themes of exile and slavery, followed by eventual justice and divine deliverance as God steps into history as a response to human suffering, find their way into the Haggadah. Abraham's idol-worshipping ancestors emerge as central figures. Present, too, are his descendants who go down to Egypt and inherit Abraham's destiny of enslavement. They cry out to God for help. The degrading servitude the Israelites endure in Egypt and the enemies of later generations who attempt to destroy them recall God's prediction, as does the liberation of the slaves. There are sacrifices too, referencing the slaughtered lamb that, at the last moment, replaces Abraham's son Isaac on his sacrificial altar, bearing witness to Abraham's fidelity and God's compassion.

There is no one single festival of Passover in the Bible, no one single authoritative account of how it used to be done originally and correctly. But there are multiple variations on a Passover (*pesach*) ritual found in the books of Exodus, Leviticus, Numbers, Deuteronomy, Joshua, I Kings, II Kings, I Chronicles and II Chronicles, Ezra, and Ezekiel.[3] These variations are all symbolically present in the meal the Haggadah liturgy comes to orchestrate. The paradigmatic biblical sources for a Passover ritual are found in Exodus 12:1–20. On the verge of the departure of the Israelites from Egypt, God tells Moses and Aaron to relay that at twilight on the eve of fourteenth day of Nisan, families must sacrifice a perfect yearling lamb, smearing its blood on their doors with branches of hyssop. Lamb's blood is the sign for the Angel of Death to pass over (Passover!) their houses when the firstborn children of the Egyptians are slain in a tenth plague. This food practice is set in a domestic context, involving the participation of the whole family, hovering watchfully over a lamb. Families (or combined households) are to roast their lambs over the fire and eat them with unleavened bread and with bitter herbs. (Hardly the seder we know and love, but it is already beginning to sound familiar.) There is a dress code of sorts: clothes secured for travel, sandals, and a staff ready in hand for the next day's hasty departure. The dress is symbolic as well as practical, suggesting that this ritual meal, marking the protection of the endangered firstborn sons in the houses of the Israelites, also prepares the slaves for their new identity as sojourners. This one-time ritual is called, in retrospect, the Passover in Egypt, as opposed to the subsequent Passover that was kept annually.

Even before this hurried meal is consumed and the horrible night of waiting to depart begins, the Israelites learn something astonishing. For the rest of all time, they will be remembering both a ritual they have yet to perform and a liberation they have yet to experience. Before surviving a harrowing escape, enduring trials during the years of desert wandering, and coming into a promised land, even before they have performed the ritual even once, they are instructed to prepare to commit it to memory and to repeat it for all of time. This anticipated practice of a less hurried, symbolic meal is called the Passover of the Generations. Fusing one ritual for now, and one for the time to come, presages, as David Stern puts it, a "dramatic collapsing of time—past, present, and future—that . . . marks much of the inner dynamics of both the seder and the Haggadah as they subsequently develop."[4]

The Passover of the Generations, celebrated in remembrance of being brought out of Egypt, is marked by seven days of eating unleavened bread in a leaven-free house. It is also referred to as the Feast of Matzot (unleavened bread), calling up the spring wheat harvest. The timing of the festival, at "the beginning of the months . . . the first of the months of the year" (Exodus 12:2), as well as elements of sacrifice and purity practices that might augur an auspicious year to come, call up the festival's linkages to ancient Near Eastern New Year celebrations.

Mount Sinai is the setting for the next Passover narration in the Hebrew Bible. On the fourteenth day of Nisan, "at twilight, there shall be a Passover offering to the Lord, and on the fifteenth day of that month, the Lord's Feast of Unleavened Bread" (Leviticus 23:4–6). The first and seventh days of celebration allow no work to be done as befits a sacred occasion, and all seven days require sacrifice to God. We are left to imagine how Passover is marked (or not) through the previous years of wandering until we come to a detailed description of the first Passover celebrated in the land promised to Abraham's ancestors. New distinctions marking the return home accumulate. Men need to be circumcised so they are eligible to offer the Passover sacrifice. A new Passover diet is instituted: not just unleavened bread and parched grain, but local foods—the produce of the country, a bounty meriting thanksgiving befitting this time in the agricultural year.

The book of Numbers introduces a "do-over" policy. Those who cannot meet the obligation of the Passover offering on the assigned day of Nisan, either because they are in a state of ritual impurity caused by their contact with the dead or because they are away on a journey, can make it up a month later. Fail to do so, and they are cut off from their kin (Numbers 9:13).

When Passover becomes a pilgrimage holiday, it is set at the Temple in Jerusalem, the home of God and the cultic center where sacred practice is privileged and national power is centralized. Families leave home and head for the city, bringing firstborn lambs to be sacrificed by priests in the Temple precincts. Afterward, family groupings eat the roasted lamb along with matzah: "You shall cook and eat it at the place that the Lord your God will choose; and in the morning you may start back on your journey home" (Deuteronomy 16:7). In the Temple, the Levites chant psalms of praise and rejoicing. Their psalms provide the first liturgical materials the Haggadah draws on, and their musicianship presages the spirit of song that will eventually characterize the seder.

Passover observance at the Temple is the occasion for large-scale revivals, drawing attention to the national aspect of the celebration. Passovers in Jerusalem sponsored by King Hezekiah (reigning in the late eighth and early seventh centuries BCE) and King Josiah (reigning from about 641 to 609 BCE) are royal extravaganzas. In Hezekiah's reign (II Chronicles 31:1–27), a great crowd reassembles for a Temple celebration a month late; the "second chance" policy is invoked. It lasts not one but two weeks, and the Levites slaughter thousands on thousands of bulls and sheep. Rejoicing is unrestrained, as this has apparently not happened, it is claimed, since the time of Solomon. King Josiah then affirms his own power when it is his turn to sponsor Passover as a national unity holiday, assuring that all of Israel, those of the north and south, keep the outdoor communal meal. His Majesty's largesse could not have gone unnoticed: he donates thirty thousand lambs and goats for the Passover offerings, and three thousand cattle. With singers at their stations, Levites (doing double duty as chefs and servers) "roasted the Passover sacrifice in fire . . . while the sacred offerings they cooked in pots, cauldrons and pans, and conveyed them with dispatch to all the people" (II Chronicles 35:13). The appraisal is again hyperbolic, and competitively so: since the time of Samuel, "no Passover like that had ever been kept in Israel: none of the kings of Israel had kept a Passover like the one kept by Josiah" (II Chronicles 35:18). How clearly the new and improved circumstances are linked to the old ways, yet there are changes. When kings are concerned, we do not hear concern about the efficaciousness or permissibility of their Passover innovations. They reflect their power and also the capaciousness and flexibility of this holiday, a sensibility the Haggadah will incorporate.

Mishnah and Tosefta: Passover, after the Temple's Destruction

The sources of the Haggadah are found not just in the Bible, but in the Mishnah, Tosefta, Talmuds (of Jerusalem and Babylonia), and Midrash. The Mishnah was set down in writing in the Land of Israel under Roman rule at the end of the second century and the beginning of the third; the Tosefta, compiled around 220 CE, includes supplementary teachings. The term Midrash (compiled between 200 and 1000 CE) refers to the rabbinic interactions with the Bible that are of both a legal (*halakha*) and a sermonic (*aggada*) nature. The Jerusalem and Babylonian Talmuds, compiled in the fifth and sixth centuries respectively, offer conversational scholarly reflections on the Mishnah that include debates on law, demands for precision and standards, chronicles of practices, and many digressions. These are oral traditions of rabbinic deliberation; when they were eventually redacted and written down, an enduring conversation speaking across generations was created, one that remains alive today.

After the Romans' destruction of the Second Temple in 70 CE, there was no longer a place to assemble for Passover pilgrimage, no place for the Levites to sacrifice the lambs at meals of celebration, remembrance, and instruction. Without those lambs, the ancestral "condiments"—that is, the matzah and bitter herbs—might have been seen as culinary signs of divine impotence, designating rupture of the covenant. But they were not eliminated; they were repurposed to prompt new narratives, ones in which the enslavement of the past could suggest that the God who redeemed Israel before might do so once again.

Rabbinic sages forged new practices, maintaining continuity with the past through encounters with text, seen as a source of ongoing revelation. Through study, deliberation, and debate, generations of rabbis needed to develop alternative ceremonies so that Jews could continue to experience connection to God. At Passover, what could still stimulate the telling of the story of the Exodus and its redemption? What could protect against a desperate feeling of abandonment by God in times of exile or despair? The symbolic service of study and ritualized dining that developed was set at a new altar. Not the synagogue or study house, but the home table. (Actually, these were probably first like the minitables brought in and out to dining patricians of Roman Palestine.) Possibly, the rabbis anticipated that being aware of Passover observances taking place simultaneously in other households might cultivate the feeling of connectedness and peoplehood[5]—what Victor and Edith Turner called communitas—once known by pilgrims assembling together.[6]

The rabbis' efforts to reconstruct Passover did not come about overnight; these efforts took years to coalesce. Ritual changes responding to loss and trauma with resilience rarely emerge all of a piece and garner wide embrace; it's a process, a messy one. There is inevitably dig-in-your-heels debate, personality conflict, power play, ritual trial and error. And Passover was no exception. Consider that in our own time it took fourteen years for the National September 11th Memorial Museum to be established because of the complex challenges of honoring different groups, including families of victims, first responders, Wall Street neighbors of many traditions, and even political stakeholders such as the Port Authority of New York and the city of New York.

What we do know is this: in the first centuries after the destruction of the Temple, there was still no definitive Haggadah, no written script explaining what to do and what to say. Lawrence Hoffman maintains that "the entire liturgy was orally delivered. We should abandon the search for an original (and therefore authentic) text; celebrants followed the structure of the night's drama without being bound by it."[7] Nonetheless, we can still trace strands of its development.

The Tosefta revealed an ad hoc Passover home ceremony taking place between 70 and 200 CE and beyond. It was briefer and less elaborate than the one found in the Mishnah's and may even have come first, as Judith Hauptman has argued.[8] The Tosefta ceremony began with a blessing over wine. (Why wine? Perhaps to make the members of the household happy enough to think about redemption. Rabbi Judah specified: women and children should be gladdened with what is "appropriate" for them—which is what? Hard to say!) Following an hors d'oeuvre of dipped sweetbreads, a few psalms were recited at the table. If no one in the household could recite the psalms, they were to make their way to the synagogue to hear them, in part, and to return after the meal for the remainder. At the table, matzah was divvied up, and bitter lettuce was dipped into charoset. Then the meal. If there were specific words to be said at the table, the Tosefta did not record them. This meal could *not* be concluded with an afikomen, then described as a trail mix dessert of nuts, dates, and roast corn. Instead, there was the just-desert of an all-night, all-male study session that lasted until the cock crowed. Instructions took into consideration varying social scenarios: "A person must engage in the laws of Pesach all night, even if it is just him and his son, even if it is just by himself, and even between him and his student."[9] Ideally, sober and awake.

The contents of the study session of the Tosefta went without saying: it was the curriculum of all the laws of Passover that learned people presumably already knew. However, it was not meant to be a conventional lecture; there should be a dialogue. Or, as Michael Walzer writes, "Perhaps we should say simply that the covenant is carried forward on a flood of talk: argument and analysis, folkloric expansion, interpretation and reinterpretation."[10]

The Mishnah (Pesachim 10) presented a more elaborate ceremony than the Tosefta. With its fixed step-by-step instructions, blessings, psalms (the selection referred to as Hallel), scripted and improvised give-and-take exchanges over Torah, God, and history, it presaged the Haggadah's arrangement of components as well as its contents. The table ritual of the Mishnah, like that of the Tosefta, called up the etiquette and table fellowship of the Greco-Roman symposium. At such banquets there were servants pouring and mixing wine and serving hors d'oeuvres, dips, sandwiches with lettuce, and multiple courses of delectable foods. There was learned discourse, satisfying conversation, formal toasting, reclining on couches arranged about the room, and handwashing. Despite such commonalities, the rabbinic version was short on revelry and inebriation. (This happens when you eliminate instrumental music, garlands, perfumes, dancers, jugglers, paramours of both sexes, and the *epikomion*, the postprandial dessert-hopping visit to other neighborhood symposia.) The rabbinic version did, at least, have its own subdued niceties. There were blessings said over four cups of wine, dipped greens, the matzah, grace after meals, and Hallel. It was democratic, too. All Jews could be present, not just the elite and wealthy, and not just adult men.

Symposium-like features, such as reclining, drinking, and discourse running through a meal, clearly also characterize the meal in the Christian tradition known as Jesus's Last Supper, in which Jesus reveals to his disciples the new meanings for the wine and the bread after his death. Thus,

> When the hour came, Jesus and his apostles reclined at the table. And he said to them, "I have eagerly desired to eat this Passover with you before I suffer. For I tell you, I will not eat it again until it finds fulfillment in the kingdom of God." After taking the cup, he gave thanks and said, "Take this and divide it among you. For I tell you I will not drink again from the fruit of the vine until the kingdom of God comes." (Luke 22:14–18)

Scholars of ancient Judaism and early Christianity vigorously debate whether this meal, the template for the Eucharist, was indeed a Passover seder, as it is often portrayed to be. Most days, I tend to side with those who are persuaded that it was not. There is the matter of timing: the three synoptic Gospels (Matthew, Mark, and Luke) agree that the Last Supper was held only *after* the Jewish holiday of Passover had begun. Jonathan Klawans notes as well that "during this meal the disciples reclined, ate both bread and wine, and sang a hymn. While such behavior may have been characteristic of the Passover meal, it is equally characteristic of any Jewish meal." Further, "the only foods we are told the disciples ate are bread and wine—the basic elements of any formal Jewish meal. If this was a Passover meal, where is the

Passover lamb? Where are the bitter herbs? Where are the four cups of wine?"[11]

There are more questions: If the Last Supper was not a seder, why were early Christian texts connecting and distinguishing it from the Jewish Passover meal? Another question: did the rabbis shape the developing seder as a polemical response to early Christianity? It's hard to imagine the rabbis being motivated to do this, as there was not yet a full-fledged seder in the time of Jesus.[12]

Returning to the differences between the Passover ceremonies of the Tosefta and Mishnah, we can see how the Mishnah provided fine tuning. Consider the placement of the study session. In the Tosefta, study came at the very end, almost as an afterthought, for men who already had their fill of wine. In the Mishnah, study came before the meal when children were still wide awake and adults more attentive. Study was the evening's centerpiece for the whole family, a main course of words, and the form of nourishment that replaced the paschal lamb and constituted a substitute form of worship. If the Tosefta offered laws, the Mishnah offered an open-ended curriculum of questions, answers, and storytelling. It assumed there was an intelligent son who would ask good questions without prodding. If the son failed to take the initiative, the father got the narrative ball rolling by pointing out four observations: (1) This night is different from all other nights; (2) on other nights, we dip once, but on this night, twice; (3) on other nights, leavened bread and matzah are eaten, but on this night, only matzah; (4) on other nights, meat is served roasted, stewed, or boiled, but tonight it is only roasted. (When we compare these early questions to those that became codified Haggadah later, aside from order, we see that the main difference is that the fourth question about roasted meat is replaced by, "On all other nights we may eat either while sitting or leaning; on this night we all eat while leaning.") The father portrayed in the Mishnah instructed his son, according to his capacity for learning, to develop his eye and mind on Passover by questioning. He rewarded his son's good observations with complex explanations, setting the stage for a formation that encouraged noticing, asking, challenging, and debating.

The Mishnah promoted engaging productively with older Passover symbols in order to keep their meanings from becoming obscure and irrelevant. Rabban Gamaliel the Younger (sometimes written as Gamliel) declared, "Whoever does not mention these three things on Passover does not discharge his duty, and they are: the Passover-offering, unleavened bread, and bitter herbs (Mishnah Pesachim 10.5). One fulfilled the duty of Passover by looking to three items on the table, speaking about them, and interpreting them anew. Attention was strategically diverted from yearning for past rituals and past times of sovereignty. The paschal lamb now referred only to the memory of God's passing over their ancestors' homes in Egypt. The bitter herbs, no longer recalled as the condiment eaten with the lamb, were repurposed as reminders of the Egyptians who embittered their ancestors' lives. The matzah, with its multiple historical evocations, now stood for one thing alone: God's ultimate redemption. Encounter with the three symbols—that is, gesturing to them, talking about them, and eating them—pointed to gratitude and praise for what had happened in the past and what would hopefully transpire in the future.

The Mishnah was succinct. The father was told to focus on a passage from Deuteronomy 26:5: "My father was a wandering (or fugitive) Aramean" (*arami oved avi*); or as it has sometimes been interpreted, "An Aramean sought to destroy my father." (One explanation is that this is a veiled reference to the Romans—*romi*—who did indeed seek to destroy Israel.) The Mishnah assumed the father knew the rest of the verse and story by heart and could tell it so the plot moved from lowly disgrace to glorious praise to God. More than that, the Mishnah assumed the father knew how to expound on it.

Why did the Mishnah select this curious and confusing passage about the wandering Aramean that eventually became central in the Haggadah? These were the words the Israelites recited on a different holiday altogether, on Shavuot, celebrated seven weeks *after* Passover. The Israelite farmers making this declaration were free people who had been returned to their own land. For the barley harvest, they converged on the Temple in Jerusalem as pilgrims to offer a first fruit sacrifice from their crops in gratitude to God for the land and its bounty. The priest in charge took their baskets and set them down for God in front of an altar. The people declared:

> My father was a wandering Aramean. He went down to Egypt with meager numbers and sojourned there; but there he became a great and very populous nation. The Egyptians dealt harshly with us and oppressed us; they imposed hard labor upon us. We cried out to the Lord, the God of our fathers, and the Lord heard our plea and saw our plight, our misery and our oppression. The Lord

freed us from Egypt by a mighty hand, by an outstretched arm, and awesome power, and by signs and with portents. (Deuteronomy 26:5–8, JPS translation)

Maybe the rabbis of the Mishnah Jews knew that these lines from the well-known, succinct telling of the Exodus story could best elicit a powerful memory of crowds gathering prayerfully together, grateful for their harvest. The last verses of the farmer's oath were pointedly omitted on Passover: "He brought us to this place and gave us this land, a land flowing with milk and honey. Wherefore I now bring the first fruits of the soil which You, O Lord, have given me" (Deuteronomy 26:9–10). Given the pain of exile, I surmise that the rabbis deleted these final verses, lest the night of Passover in exile turn into an eve of lamentations, mourning freedom having come undone, and along with it, God's covenantal promises to Abraham's descendants.

Rabbis and scholars have long pondered why this text was selected. Recently, Rabbi David Berger of Yeshiva University offered up his own granddaughter's compelling explanation, one I had never heard. She pointed out to him that it "is the only account of the bondage and exodus written in the first person. It is consequently the most appropriate choice to help fulfill the Haggadah's injunction that each person imagine that he himself came out of Egypt."[13]

Talmud

The Talmudic tractates on Passover bring us closer to an actual Haggadah, particularly with explicit reference to the obligation of "saying Haggadah."[14] It came in the context of a question. Was a blind person exempt from "saying Haggadah," given that the blind are exempt from fulfilling certain commandments for themselves or on behalf of others? The matter was resolved: the obligation of "saying Haggadah" *was* incumbent on the blind. Proof came not from a biblical passage, the usual source for authoritative evidence, but from observations drawn from real life. In this case, these were eyewitness memories of what important rabbis had been doing at their very own seders.

As the story goes, Mereimar had been told there were two blind rabbis, Rav Yosef and Rav Sheshet, who used to "say Haggadah" in their own houses, and those who heard their recitations could say that in hearing them, they, too, had fulfilled the obligation themselves. From this anecdote, we also learn that one person recited the oral text on behalf of the others. (Those in recent years who have experienced democratic seders in which everyone at the table takes a turn reading from a Haggadah should recall that the tradition of having a *ba'al haseder*—literally "master of the seder," one who recites from the Haggadah—was challenged only in modern times and is still followed in many places today.)

The Talmud supplied hints for making the ceremony successful as a teaching event. Rabbi Akiva sent the fathers in his study hall home early on the eve of Passover so they could serve their children snacks and make sure they napped. He commended them to distribute parched grain and walnuts to keep them alert. He prescribed matzah snatching (perhaps in the absence of other amusements, this was quite entertaining). The game does seem to be a precursor of the practice later linked to the afikomen, the piece of matzah that is wrapped and then snatched away by children, who bargain with their parents over its ransom so that the seder feast can come to an end with the afikomen as dessert.

The rabbis of the Talmud, whose conversations extended across generations, scrutinized every element of the Passover ceremony: the wine, the blessings, the leaning—and they differed in their understandings of rules and rationales, usually confirming the teachings of the Mishna, but not always. Three debates indicate some of the far-ranging discussion, part of the Haggadah's backstory.

The first debate was over how many cups of wine were required. The matter seemed resolved in the Mishnah: four cups. But in an early edition of the Talmud, Rabbi Tarfon was said to have recited Hallel on Passover over a fifth cup (B. Talmud Pesachim 118b). Admittedly, drinking four cups was risky, as the number four could be taken as constituting two pairs of two. And why exactly would that be a problem? There was a belief that doing anything "in pairs" (*zugot*) was unlucky and could unleash demonic forces (B. Talmud Pesachim 109a–112b). Drinking wine or beer in even numbers, making love twice, passing between a pair of women (for surely they are sorcerers!), and sitting on either side of the fork of a road: all were unlucky. Why? Simple: it was common knowledge! Some rabbis claimed a more authoritative source. They had heard it from Joseph the Demon himself, who proclaimed that the very king of demons was appointed over all pairs. Not surprisingly, different rabbis who heard Joseph the Demon interpreted him differently, and the redactor of their anxious voices led to a reasonable conclusion: exercise caution when it comes to pairs, but don't get obsessed. The evolving Haggadah accepted the majority voice: drink four cups—but beware! With the danger of pairs still lurking, a compromise position evolved: bad luck could be eradicated with a fifth cup.

Our second debate concerns how properly to narrate the Passover story (called the *maggid*, "the telling"). How should it start and how should it end; that is, what is the story line? The Mishnah advised that the Passover story should begin with disgrace and end with praise. But what exactly did disgrace and praise refer to? Rav defined disgrace as the Israelite's shame of having ancestors who once worshipped idols. Praise referred to their finally becoming free and worthy to worship the one true God. In contrast, Samuel maintained that the disgrace referred to having ancestors who suffered the lowliness of being slaves in Egypt, and praise meant Divine liberation (B. Talmud Pesachim 116a). As a consequence of a community's reading practices that honor multiple, even contradictory readings, the Haggadah came to embrace a weaving of both narratives.

Our third debate concerns charoset, the seder's fruity nut paste. Was eating it a mitzvah, a commandment? The rabbis were categorizing the rules of Passover. There were the most sacred, the commandments set down in the Torah; second in weightiness were commandments ordained by rabbis; and finally, lovely customs and practices that were once optional, and then later on, became binding. Where did charoset fit? The Mishnah had stated that charoset was not commanded by the Torah, but Rabbi Eleazar, son of Rabbi Zadok, argued that it was. Three Talmudic sages, Rabbi Levi, Rabbi Johanan, and Abaye, also maintained that charoset was commanded by the Torah. They supported their claim by turning to sources in the Torah and Midrash in which charoset's symbolic meanings evoke different and important aspects of the Exodus narrative:

> Rabbi Levi said: In memory of the apple-tree (That is, the apple trees under which the Israelite women secretly gave birth to their babies, so they would not be killed, according to Pharaoh's decree).
>
> Rabbi Johanan said: In memory of the clay (That is, the materials used by the enslaved Israelites to build bricks for Pharaoh).
>
> Abaye observed: Therefore one must make it acrid and thicken it: make it acrid, in memory of the apple-tree; and thicken it, in memory of the clay.
>
> It was taught in accordance with Rabbi Johanan: The spices are in memory of the straw (an element in brick-building); charoset is a reminder of the clay. (B. Talmud, Pesachim, 116a)

But the most irresistible proof for charoset being a mitzvah harked back to Rabbi Eleazar. He looked neither to texts nor to the sayings or practices of sages. He took to the street and observed everyday people getting ready for Passover. He heard the grocers of Jerusalem crying out from their windows, essentially saying, "Charoset! Charoset! Come and buy the spices you need for the mitzvah (commandment) of charoset!" and he watched purchases being made. Whatever other rabbis thought about the practice, Eleazar knew that in the people's eyes (and in the eyes of their grocers), the matter of charoset had been settled. Of course it was a mitzvah!

This talmudic decision asserting the weighty significance of charoset resonated in the story of Jewish soldiers from the Ohio Union Volunteer Regiment who celebrated Passover 1862 in Fayette, West Virginia. They received "Hagedahs" and seven barrels of matzahs shipped from Ohio. Lacking some of the other proper ingredients for the rest of the seder, but knowing what was essential, they improvised:

> Horseradish or parsley we could not obtain, but in lieu we found a weed, whose bitterness, I apprehend, exceeded anything our forefathers "enjoyed." We were still in a great quandary; we were like the man who drew the elephant in the lottery. We had the lamb, but did not know what part was to represent it at the table; but Yankee ingenuity prevailed, and it was decided to cook the whole and put it on the table, then we could dine off it, and be sure we had the right part. The necessaries for the choroutzes we could not obtain, so we got a brick which, rather hard to digest, reminded us, by looking at it, for what purpose it was intended.[15]

Midrash

Midrash unpacks perplexing aspects of the biblical texts and clarifies them by creatively bringing other texts from the Bible and elsewhere in the tradition into conversation. (Midrash refers to particular collections of exegesis as well as to the technique of engaging imaginatively with sacred Jewish texts that continues to be used by rabbis and even artists and writers to this day.) The interplay of linking verses, even those taken out of context, and forging interpretations has become a hallmark of the Haggadah and one of its primary teaching techniques.

One well-known consequence of midrashic activity that appears in the Haggadah is the passage about four sons who ask about the meaning of Passover. (Feminist interventions in recent Haggadot have rendered these archetypal characters as both sons and daughters or as children.) The Bible makes it clear that the parent is responsible to teach and transmit the memory of Exodus; it is the core curriculum for cultural reproduction. That said, why does the Bible state this four times and in different ways?[16] Midrash accounts for these redundancies, not only justifying them, but, in the process, also imparting a lesson well known to the best teachers: if you want your teaching to be effective, you have to adapt your curriculum to where your students are at. Making this point, the midrashic imagination creates four different sons, each with a different character: the wise, the wicked, the simple (in some sources, he was downright stupid), and the one whose mind was such a tabula rasa that he did not even know how to formulate, let alone pose, a question. While the Haggadah will claim that the Torah actually refers to these four children who ask about the meaning of Passover, no such actual figures exist.

Let us look at how midrash addresses just one of the four biblical passages through the creation of the wise son. In the Haggadah, he is given to ask a question posed in Deuteronomy 6:20: "What are the decrees, laws and rules that the Lord our God has enjoined upon you?" In the biblical context, this hypothetical question gets a long and satisfying answer. It brings in history, an abridged guide to ritual and pragmatic rationales for practice, leading to reverence, survival, and merit:

> We were slaves to Pharaoh in Egypt and the Lord freed us from Egypt with a mighty hand. The Lord wrought before our eyes marvelous signs and portents in Egypt, against Pharaoh and all his household, and He freed us from there, that He might take us and give us the land that He had promised on oath to our fathers. Then the Lord commanded us to observe all these laws, to revere the Lord our God, for our lasting good and for our survival, as it is now the case. It will be therefore to our merit before the Lord our God to observe faithfully this whole instruction as He has commanded us. (Deuteronomy 6:21–25)

But this is not the answer the Haggadah's wise son gets. In keeping with his imagined studiousness, piety, and acquiescence, the midrash teaches him all the laws of Passover, including a rule *not* to eat afikomen. (In this particular context, afikomen refers not to a piece of hidden matzah which must be eaten at the conclusion of the ceremonial meal, but to the Greco-Roman after-dinner revelry.) Why would Torah study and ritual eating and drinking be emphasized in the answer the wise son gets? Menachem Kasher suggests it is because the wise son understands that eating fulfills God's law no less than study and prayer.[17] Thus, a son who is wise can eat his way back into Abraham's original covenant.

When did the Haggadah, with all of this rich textual backstory, start to coalesce? When did it get written down? To be sure, it was not born fully formed. It is to that part of Haggadah's life that we now turn.

On Becoming a Book

From the Earliest Haggadot to the Illuminated Haggadot of the Middle Ages

Agnes Lewis and Margaret Gibson were Scottish Presbyterian identical twin sisters, scholars who had become accustomed to adventuresome travel on camel through the Middle East searching for ancient sacred texts. They had returned home to Cambridge in May 1896 and were paying a call on Solomon Schechter at Cambridge University, inviting the professor of rabbinic literature to examine beguiling documents they had acquired from the Ezra Synagogue in Fustat in Old Cairo. They had been retrieved from the synagogue's genizah, a repository housing the community's worn Hebrew manuscripts. Intrigued by what else might be found, Schechter set off to Cairo on an exploratory expedition of his own, returning to Cambridge with sacks holding thousands of documents. These included pages and fragments of various Haggadah texts.[1]

The earliest more or less complete ones were traced to Amram Gaon (ninth century) and Saadya Gaon (tenth century), rabbinic heads (*geonim*) of the academies for Jewish learning that had grown up in the Babylonian cities of Sura and Pumpedita. They had not come from freestanding Haggadot; compilations of the Haggadah as a book did not come into being until the thirteenth century. They had come from books of prayer composing the entire year's liturgy that the *geonim* had assembled for Jews around the world.

Schechter retrieved four hundred Haggadah fragments reflecting the tradition of Babylonia and forty representing the diverse variations of the tradition of Eretz Yisrael (the Land of Israel). One fragment from a codex of the Eretz Yisrael tradition had already been looted from the genizah before Professor Schechter appeared. It was then sold to a law professor and bibliophile who donated it to Dropsie College of Philadelphia, and hence its name, the "Dropsie Haggadah" (it now resides at the University of Pennsylvania). Similar to other versions of the Eretz Yisrael tradition, this fragment is close in content to the ceremony that was proposed in the Mishnah, and in it, verses of the Mishnah are reframed as Passover liturgy. The Dropsie Haggadah is comparatively short, with only three questions about what makes the night of Passover different, and no mention of the Four Sons. Its explanations are pointed; midrashic diversion are held in check. This Haggadah does include something unique: a potpourri of blessings for different kinds of foods eaten at the seder's outset. Imagine a seder begun, not with a single sad sprig of saltwater-dipped parsley or even Amram's selection of lettuce, celery, or cilantro, but with a tempting array of hors d'oeuvres—elaborate dips involving "rice, mixed with eggs and honey; dates, figs or grapes; sweetbreads and skewers of grilled meats and sausages . . . !"[2] In fact, Jewish educators today, keen on fore-stalling impatience-induced hunger of children (and adults alike) at the seder, point to the culinary precedent of the Dropsie Haggadah, validating their suggestion that a seder should begin with substantial hors d'oeuvres, or at the very least, crudités and dips.

Recall: in the Mishnaic period one fulfilled the Pass-over's obligations by teaching children, engaging with the festival's symbolic foods outlined by Rabban Gamaliel, and reciting psalms. As the Haggadah was written down, com-petition emerged among rabbis who sought to press for the authority of their versions. In the mid-ninth century, Rabbi Natronai, head of the academy of Sura, demonstrated his au-thority when he passionately defended the Babylonian Hag-gadah traditions over those of Eretz Yisrael. He rebuked those who failed to embrace his version, claiming that those who didn't follow it had failed to observe the obligations of Passover. (In particular, he castigated the Karaites, calling them heretics who disdained rabbinic interpretation and said they deserved to be excommunicated.)

If additions were important for the proponents of the Babylonian tradition, omissions were too, especially when they might reduce the despair of an exilic community. In his tenth-century Haggadah text, part of a siddur (prayer book), Saadya pointedly omitted a biblical passage referring to a return to the promised land, so as to draw attention away from the rival existing community in the land of Israel and to affirm the status of his community in Babylonia.

By the eleventh century, the Haggadah was becoming consolidated, but it still did not possess all the spelled-out contents deemed nowadays as "traditional."[3] Householders were assumed to know how to prepare for the seder from oral transmission and experience; they didn't need written instruction or directions for assembling the seder's symbolic foods. (A special seder plate for these foods was not created until the sixteenth century.) They were assumed to know how to prepare their homes for the holiday and search them symbolically beforehand for unleavened bread. (In the medieval period, benedictions were composed to signify that leaven inadvertently left behind should be considered "null and void.")

At first, there was not the now familiar rhyming mnemonic, *Simanei haseder shel pesach* (signs of the order of Passover), to provide a preview at the outset of the seder of what steps were to come and to mark progress as one went along. Attributed to the thirteenth-century Rabbi Samuel ben Solomon of Falaise, France, the steps were written down, and they have been followed ever since:

> Kadesh: Recite the blessing over wine
> U'rechatz: Wash hands, without the blessing
> Karpas: Recite the blessing over a green vegetable
> Yachatz: Break the middle matzah
> Maggid: Tell the story of Passover
> Rachtzah: Wash hands, saying the blessing
> Motzi: Say the prayer for the beginning of the meal
> Matzah: Recite the blessing over the matzah
> Maror: Recite the blessing over the bitter herbs
> Korech: Make and eat the sandwich named after
>   Rabbi Hillel
> Shulchan Orech: Eat the festive meal
> Tzafun: Find and eat the afikomen

Barech: Say grace
Hallel: Recite psalms and prayers
Nitzah: Conclude the seder[4]

The lengthier Babylonian text was widely disseminated. Jews in different communities adapted it and they, in turn, further developed versions they had received, reflecting regional rites of Jews of Ashkenaz (France and Germany), Sepharad (the Iberian Peninsula), Yemen, and elsewhere. The text, with its regional variations, remained more or less stable until the nineteenth century, though it was expanded on with songs, religious poems (*piyyutim*), and commentaries.[5]

In the medieval period, Moses Maimonides, called the Rambam, was the source of essential writing on Passover observance. Rabbi, philosopher, and physician, he was born in Cordoba, Spain, in 1138 and lived out his last years in Fustat, Cairo. He prayed at the Ezra synagogue, the site of the Cairo genizah, and writings in his own hand were discovered in Schechter's cache. It was in Fustat that Maimonides wrote the *Mishneh Torah*, the code clarifying and explaining each Jewish commandment. His chapters on the Passover commandments resolved practical questions about seder proceedings. What exactly counts as a bitter herb? According to Maimonides, fresh lettuce, endive, horseradish, chicory, and dandelion are all fine; have an olive's worth of one, or a mixture of them. It is also fine to eat the dried stalks, "but if one stews, pickles, or cooks them, he has not fulfilled his duty."[6] Maimonides also addressed theological and pedagogical issues the written Haggadah opens up, some that continue to be perplexing.

One such question is still asked: Why does the heroic biblical figure of Moses make negligible appearances in the

Haggadah? Shouldn't he be the hero of the story, like Esther of Purim, Judah Maccabee of Hanukkah? Maimonides wrote that it was up to parents to decide just how present Moses should be in the story. For young or foolish children, better to gloss over the complicated matter of why an all-powerful God would need to turn to a human being such as Moses for help. It was enough to tell such children that if not for God's rescue, they wouldn't be sitting here at the seder table today and would still be enslaved. To bring the point home, Maimonides suggested pointing to one's own maid and manservant as exemplars of those who had been dealt a bitter fate. But intelligent children could indeed comprehend that help from a man as great as Moses hardly diminished God's power. In this advanced curriculum, parents "should tell everything that happened to us in Egypt, and the miracles wrought for us by the hand of our teacher Moses."[7] Stories about the role of Moses were thus not really excluded; it was just assumed that parents would know them well enough to narrate them appropriately to their offspring.

Maimonides's writings on Passover included his own authoritative Haggadah text. He described it as "current in Israel during the present exile."[8] The experience of exile was readily recalled early in the seder, in the section called *maggid*, in which the story of Exodus is briefly told as the matzot are lifted. Maimonides interjected, "We left Egypt in a hurry," and then continued with a clear yearning for return:

> This is the bread of poverty which our ancestors ate in the land of Egypt.
> All who are hungry, let them come in and eat.

All who are needy, let them come and celebrate the Passover.

This year we are here; next year may we be in the land of Israel.

This year we are slaves; next year may we be free.

MEDIEVAL ILLUMINATED HAGGADOT

By the fourteenth century in Sepharad, and by the fifteenth century in Ashkenaz, the Haggadah was becoming an object one owned—sometimes in multiple copies—and it took on the life of a personal ritual object. It was used for the Passover holiday and was possibly referenced year-round because it contained table blessings that were recited for other festivals. Having a text in hand allowed for scholarly conversation among those adept at explicating the Haggadah according to the prescribed exegetical principles: the *peshat* (plain meaning); *remez* (deeper level of meaning); *derash* (interpretation, or homily); and *sod* (secret, or mystical meaning). One might imagine that young people felt their maturity was recognized when they were given the privilege of holding a hand-copied Haggadah in their hands for the first time.

The eventual introduction of decoration and imagery into the Haggadah maintained its fluidity in this era. Artistry changed the way that a Haggadah, as an object, was handled and gazed at. When the artistry pushed beyond embellishment, it fostered flexible interpretations and extended Judaic literacy. For certain, Haggadot of particular beauty increased the joy of the holiday and may have

burnished an owner's social status as well. Dedicatory in-
scriptions indicate that they were made for the commission-
er's own use as well as for gifts to family members on special
occasions, such as a wedding.

Prior to the eleventh and twelfth centuries, as far as we
know, the only visual elements in Haggadah texts were decorative doodle-like scribal motifs for the bitter herbs and
matzah. The historian Cecil Roth once speculated that
given how fully realized the drawings were in the Haggadot
of the fourteenth century, and given how Haggadot became
primary sites for Jewish artistic expression in the twelfth and
thirteenth centuries, there may have been an "anterior tradition" of adding visual elements that had been lost due to
"the vicissitudes of Jewish history (that) resulted in a vast
destruction of books of all types." Could there have been a
Jewish tradition of illuminated manuscripts that was "inter-
rupted in the Orient by the rise of iconophobic tendencies"
and then resumed in the Occident? Roth lamented that in
the late 1960s only "two or three" people were interested in
the history of Jewish art as much as he was. He chortled
about how narrow the boundaries of Jewish study were in
his day, writing: "Art has not taken its place among the disci-
plines of the major *yeshivot* (schools of sacred text learning)
and kindred bodies."[9] These days, there is abundant scholarship on Jewish art.

Wealthy Jewish families commissioned artists and Hebrew scribes with fine hands to create beautiful Haggadot.
In places in Europe where Jews were said to have been excluded from artists' guilds, Christian artists in secular work-
shops were sometimes instructed by Jewish patrons (with
advice of rabbis) to create the images for the Haggadah.

Whether the artists were Jewish or Christian, they were exposed to Christian images and illuminating techniques. In particular, traditions of layout, including decorations of initial words, full-page miniatures, and marginal decorations, were resources for Jewish expression.[10] Unlike Christian Bibles with images meant to teach the illiterate, illuminated Haggadot generally assumed readers were familiar with the Bible and popular midrashic interpretations. Further, for Jewish readers, the Haggadah's images were not intended as icons, fostering devotion through a practice of visual meditation. Adding images to a Haggadah was motivated by a principle called *hiddur mitzvah*, enhancing a commanded practice (in this case, telling the Passover story) with beauty.

In the fourteenth century, images in Haggadot were neither mere embellishments nor literal and straightforward illustrations of the Passover story and seder practices. They were the text's visual partners, serving as both "countertext and commentary,"[11] in the words of Marc Epstein, a historian of Haggadah art. By interpolating the relationship between texts and images, including those revealing the everyday lives of Jews of their period and place, we can understand how the collaboration of patron, scribe, artist, and rabbinical advisor reveals information about their acclimation to the culture in which they lived and their aspirations for a better life. Notably, struggles and yearnings of the day might have been covertly expressed when they were mapped onto those of the oppressed and then redeemed Israelites.

Volumes of illuminated Haggadot of this era that were created in German lands, France, Italy, and in the Iberian Peninsula are now considered among Judaism's greatest treasures. Many have become available in both modest and extravagant facsimiles; many are now digitized and can be studied in detail (see "Resources" herein). Here, we focus on three well-known and charismatic masterpieces: The Birds' Head, the Sarajevo, and the Washington Haggadot. All have had dramatic lives (the first two, especially) and have displayed great resilience. One can only hope that their vulnerable years are behind them.

Birds' Head Haggadah

It was a summer day long after Passover had past, and I was paying a visit to the Birds' Head Haggadah, the earliest illuminated Haggadah we have.[12] With appropriate honor, it was displayed in the newly designed Morton Mandel Wing for Jewish Art and Life of the Israel Museum in Jerusalem. It was in the company of other rare medieval and Renaissance manuscripts arranged in a semicircle, all lit as treasures in a darkened crypt. I overheard a guide impressing on his tour group that the Birds' Head Haggadah was a gem, one of the museum's most treasured and iconic objects. I was therefore surprised that the tourists took but an obedient peek at the Birds' Head and then quickly flocked over to the nearby Nuremberg Mahzor, written in 1301. I took a quick look at the Mahzor myself and understood why they kept on ogling at it even after their guide tried to scurry them onward. The Mahzor, a community prayer book for the entire year, was a massive 50 × 37 cm work containing 1,042 pages, and it was embellished with elaborate and refined golden initial words. It's the kind of grand artifact that takes your breath away.

So I returned to the Birds' Head, all 27 × 18.2 centimeters of it, and had it all to myself. Created in the Rhineland around the year 1300, it was written in dark brown ink on parchment by a scribe named Menachem, which we know because he marked the consonants of his name in the text. Along the way, the Birds' Head Haggadah got its name from what appear to be its hallmark grotesque birds' heads, each with a personality of its own. The curious cartoon-like heads are carried atop the bodies of Jews: Moses, Aaron, and the Israelites who are shown sustained by one Germanic eagle-looking quail and disks of multicolored manna dropped from two hands emerging from a cloud hovering over the desert. The birds' heads are also attached to people celebrating Passover. Wearing medieval dress, they are busy rolling, pricking, and baking matzahs; even a child with a birds' head who dutifully returns the afikomen to his bird-headed father. Earlier scholars often assumed that the birds' heads were a strategy for avoiding using human likenesses in a holy text, a way to skirt around the second commandment. (This commandment concerning a prohibition against making graven images has come to be differently understood. It does not so much prohibit the artistic creation of human likenesses as it does the worship of those images.)

The Birds' Head Haggadah contains four of the different categories of images that became standard in illuminated Haggadah manuscripts, then in printed ones, and then in later illuminated revivals of the eighteenth century. In the first category, there are illustrations of the Exodus stories that are explicitly referenced in the Haggadah, coming from the Bible—such as the ten plagues. The Haggadah's midrashic stories are also illustrated with many renditions of both the

FIGURE 2.1. Birds' Head Haggadah.

four sons and the four rabbis, deep in discussion, whose seder would never have ended had their students not told them that morning had come. In the second category, there are illustrations of Passover rituals. These include preparing the house for the Passover seder, baking matzahs (figure 2.1), pounding charoset, drinking wine, presenting and eating the symbolic foods of the seder, washing hands, and sitting down for the meal. (In the Birds' Head, we see great precision in demonstrating exactly how to go about combining the matzah with other foods and making a sandwich.) Whole families engage in the appropriate preparations and, in some Haggadot, women are shown seated at the seder table with their own books in hand. As one might imagine, celebrants are dressed appropriately for their own period, and their dining rooms are outfitted with the furniture, holiday foods, place settings, and lighting of their time and place. In the third category are illustrations from outside the Haggadah. These depict biblical stories that are alluded to in the Haggadah but are not specifically mentioned, such as scenes from the early life of Moses. They might go back even farther, as many Sephardic Haggadot did, with the key stories of Genesis in miniature. The biblical scenes of the Sarajevo Haggadah, which we will consider below, go all the way up to the death of Moses, which takes place before the Israelites make their way into the land of Canaan. In the final category there are eschatological illustrations, those depicting the end of days. These include images of the coming of the prophet Elijah who heralds the coming of the Messiah, of the righteous in paradise, and of a rebuilt, heavenly Jerusalem.

The images of the Birds' Head reveal the world its creator inhabited. There was the backdrop of Jews accused of heresy, blood libel, and the murder of Christian children in the preparation of matzahs. Epstein suggests that the birds' heads that grace the Jewish figures are intended as signs of nobility, meant to counter Christian depictions of Jews performing ritual murders. He maintains the heads on top of the Jewish characters are heads of griffins—imaginary creatures that are part lion, part eagle, akin to the sphinx. Griffin heads were a particularly apt way to portray a noble image of the Jews of Mainz, who had been described "as leonine and aquiline in addition to human."[13] The use of animals' heads could have been an interpretive strategy that allowed the readers of this Haggadah to imagine Jews themselves—despite their everyday social and economic marginalization—as individuals who possessed agency and were able to overcome the base depictions of Jews of their day. Even the cone-shaped hats that the male figures wear can be interpreted not as signs of being forced to display their Jewish identities but as evidence that they wore their distinctiveness proudly and transmitted it successfully to the next generation, just as their ancestors had done. This is most evident in the last miniature of this Haggadah, where hat-wearing, griffin-headed youthful Jewish men dressed in traveling capes point upward toward Jerusalem. This image, alongside the written text, "Next year in Jerusalem," discloses that Jerusalem is not a symbol of distant redemption, a heavenly Jerusalem of the spiritual imagination, but a literal possibility hopefully around the bend.

We know something about the provenance of the Birds' Head and its life as an object from the signatures of its owners. From one Samson Bibatz, by the nineteenth century, it passed to the Benedikt family. Johanna Benedikt married Dr. Ludwig Marum of Karlsruhe, a Jewish German politician who opposed the Nazi party. He was deported to the Kisslau concentration camp and perished there in 1934. Somehow the Haggadah parted from Marum's wife and daughters, who immigrated to France and survived their own internment there. A Jewish refugee in Karlsruhe named Hermann Kahn came to possess the Haggadah; it's not sure how. He sold it for $600 in 1946 to the Bezalel Museum, which eventually became the Israel Museum; there, its significance was recognized. Most recently, after seeing the Haggadah exhibited at the museum, descendants of the Marum family have challenged the legality of Kahn's ownership and his right to have sold what they claim as their property that was stolen by the Nazis. The Marum family is represented by American attorney E. Randol Schoenberg, portrayed in the 2015 film *Woman in Gold* for having helped Maria Altmann to recover her family's five stolen Gustav

Klimt paintings. The Marum family is willing to allow the museum to continue exhibiting the Haggadah, but they want compensation and want to be named as the owners. The situation remains, at this writing, still unresolved.

Sarajevo Haggadah

As Haggadot moved alongside their Jewish owners into the uncertain fates associated with expulsions and multiple exiles, it is remarkable that any Haggadah of the medieval era had the fortune to survive. But the Sarajevo Haggadah did—over and again. This small (22 × 16 cm) parchment codex of bleached calfskin was, in all likelihood, created in Barcelona, probably by a Jewish artist, sometime between 1350 and 1370. Its first thirty-four pages are beguilingly illuminated in gold, copper, and jewel-like colors; fifty pages that follow are devoted to text. Like other Sephardic Haggadot of the era, it begins with biblical miniatures. The images of the Sarajevo Haggadah are inspired by both the Latin Bible illumination practices of the Franco-Spanish school and the Italian gothic style. Figures dressed as Spaniards of the day enact a précis of the Bible's central narratives, from the creation of the world to the family dramas of Genesis, and eventually on to the death of Moses. These scenes are followed by images of the Temple in Jerusalem and contemporary holiday tableaux of charoset being doled out and matzah being distributed. While the inscription says, "The master of the house distributes matzah," to his family, the image depicts a democratic scene, as a whole community is receiving matzahs. Why did inventive and colorful illuminations of matzah play a significant role in this and other Spanish medieval Haggadot? It had so many symbolic meanings, representing the divine presence, Israel's election, Jewish identity, and also hope for redemption. It also referenced another popular image some Jews were aware of: the consecrated host.

We see the Sarajevo Haggadah opening up interpretive possibilities as it illustrates Jews leaving a synagogue on Passover eve, eager to return home.[14] They are led by a small boy (is that a Haggadah in his hand?) whose father lovingly pats his head and prods him along. Curiously, the synagogue's ark is open, revealing a Torah scroll, a practice that does not transpire on a Passover eve, when Torah scrolls remain stored inside the closed ark. Eva Frojmavic ventures the image is there to affirm that the "Torah of the present is the same as the Torah given at Sinai and the Torah of messianic times."[15]

Within the text itself, there are initial word panels, decorated with floral motifs, animals, dragons, and grotesques, and there are several marginal images. The meaning of one image, possibly created by a different artist, remains famously perplexing. Illuminating the text for the ritual washing of hands and the blessing over the matzah, it depicts a seder table covered in a white cloth and laden with all the holiday necessities, except Haggadot. The master of the house reclines on a pillow and drinks from his golden beaker; his son sits next to him, holding a child-sized cup. A modestly scarfed mother holds her own golden cup. One of the remaining participants is a small dark-skinned woman, possibly African? She may be a servant, as Moors served Jews at the time in Barcelona and Majorca. Perhaps she is a convert, as she appears to be observing the holiday, matzah in hand and golden cup at her place setting, and she is as well-dressed in Spanish style as the others. Or maybe she is a foreign visitor, for at the time, the image of an African was used to denote foreignness in general.

How, in practice, did those who owned the Sarajevo Haggadah experience the preface of rich illuminations in relationship to the text that followed? It is unlikely that the images were consulted by the leader or family members during the seder itself; going back and forth would have been clumsy and time consuming; besides, there are no prompts that call for turning backward for additional mid-seder edification. Most likely, the seder leader and family members enjoyed perusing the images while preparing for the holiday, or studied them together with their children during the festival week.[16]

As I suggested, this Haggadah has amazingly survived its dramatic life. It would have left Spain with the wealthy family that owned it when the Jews of Barcelona were expelled in 1492. It may have stayed with them or their ancestors as they found refuge in Portugal, accompanying them farther to the ghetto of Venice. We know this for sure: there, Hebrew books were subject to censorship by the Pope's Inquisition and were vulnerable to expurgation of theologically objectionable passages or to destruction. In 1609, when the priest Giovanni Domenico Vistorini inspected this Haggadah, without any of excision of phrases or pages, he signed that he approved it: *Revisto per mi*, meaning "surveyed by me."

The book's life from 1609 to 1894 is unclear, but its trail picks up at the end of the nineteenth century. It surfaced in Sarajevo and was sold to the Bosnian National Museum by the Kohen family, which had fallen on hard times. In one telling, the fatherless Kohen son brought the Haggadah, its family's remaining heirloom, for sale first to his primary school, and from there it went to the National Museum in Sarajevo. The museum sent it to so-called experts in Vienna who damaged it by discarding and replacing its original bindings. They declared it to be authentic and a master-piece as well; art historians celebrated it as the earliest exemplar of figurative Jewish art, something they assumed was forbidden. Word of the museum's great treasure spread to the Nazis.

The German Army entered Sarajevo, destroying synagogues, burning Torah scrolls, and deporting Jews, Gypsies, and Serb resisters. In 1941, a Nazi commander appeared at the museum's library demanding that the Haggadah be turned over to him. The chief librarian at the museum, Derviš Korkut, an Islamic scholar with well-known strong anti-Fascist views, anticipated the worst for the Haggadah and persuaded the museum's director to release it to him. The director told the Nazi commander that a German officer had already come to claim it. Korkut was then able to smuggle the book out under his coat and brought it home, endangering his wife and child. He then found shelter for the Haggadah in the village library of an imam, who hid it among Qur'ans until the war was over and it could be safely returned.

The saga continues. In 1942, Korkut sheltered Mira Papo, a Jewish girl of Spanish descent, disguising her as their Muslim servant. This also endangered his family. Years later, during the deadly Serbian siege of Sarajevo in the 1990s, Papo posthumously repaid the kindness of the Korkut family, for a written testimony he left behind paved the way for the rescue of Korkut's own daughter and her husband after Serbians' bombing turned them into refugees. They were brought to safety in Israel, at which time Korkut and his wife were recognized officially as rescuers of the Jews.

Hard to believe; there is more. The Haggadah came under threat again during the 1992 siege when the Serbs shelled the National Museum of Bosnia and Herzegovina. Enver Imamovic, director of the museum, and policemen and guards risked their lives to rescue the Haggadah and transfer it to a bank vault, where it was hidden. In 1996, one year after the partition of Bosnia by the Dayton Accords, ABC News' *Nightline* dispatched photojournalist Edward Serotta to Sarajevo to track down the hidden Haggadah, an assignment that required him to call in favors from senators and Bosnian government officials. Passover and Easter were about to start, and the journalist described his mission as a prayer for peace. *Nightline*'s host Ted Koppel introduced Serotta's mission as a quest:

> Somewhere in this war-torn city lies a medieval manuscript worth millions of dollars . . . it is called the Sarajevo Haggadah. . . . it has an aura of mystery . . . so many . . . people . . . wanted to destroy it . . . and it always survived . . . and its existence became an emblem for the entire city . . . a lot of people have been looking for it . . . tonight, "Search for Hope, the Quest for the Sarajevo Haggadah."[17]

Koppel compared finding the Haggadah to finding the ark in which the Ten Commandments were carried, or perhaps the Holy Grail. Dependent as the Haggadah had already been on people across faiths risking their lives to protect it, surely its discovery would symbolize the stubborn and heroic endurance of multicultural Bosnia. Serotta's persistence paid off. In a tiny room in a secret location, the museum director snipped the ropes and seals from a protective box, donned gloves, and gave Serotta and his *Nightline* film crew a peek at the Haggadah's fabled introductory miniatures. Serotta, inspired by his brief communion with the actual book, reflected: "The message of the Haggadah is not in the words, but in the actions they call for: to feed the hungry, to attend to those in need." And so the segment closed touchingly with images of Sarajevo's Jewish community clinic, pharmacy, and soup kitchen, a place where all, regardless of religion or ethnicity, receive care.

Writer Geraldine Brooks had heard of the Haggadah when she was covering the Bosnian war as a journalist for the *New Yorker* in the early 1990s. She narrated its dramatic life in the December 3, 2007, issue and a year later published her historical novel *People of the Book*.[18] This account of the history of the Sarajevo Haggadah introduces a romance between a fictional Australian book conservator and a museum director (and eventual Haggadah rescuer). As the conservator restores the book for exhibition, the past lives of the Sarajevo Haggadah are revealed through flashbacks that depart imaginatively from the known facts. (One invented character is Zarah, a Moorish woman who turns out to be the artist of the Haggadah; she is identified in the novel as the aforementioned African at the seder table in one of the Haggadah's miniatures.)

Brooks's novel, like Serotta's *Nightline* segment before it, emphasizes the symbolic role that the Haggadah has played across ages and cultures. One of her characters, a conservation scientist, remarks to Hanna, the conservator, that the Haggadah illustrates how fragile efforts to respect diversity and work together across cultures are:

> You've got a society where people tolerate difference, like Spain in the *Convivencia*, and everything's humming along: creative, prosperous. Then somehow this fear, this hate, this need to demonize "the other"—it just sort of rears up and smashes the whole society. Inquisition, Nazis, extremist Serb nationalists . . . same old, same old. It seems to me the book, at this point, bears witness to all that.[19]

The story still continues. A decade ago, there were media reports, confirmed by Brooks, that actress Catherine Zeta-Jones purchased film rights for Brooks's book and planned to star as the heroine (no production, so far),[20] and "A Sarajevo Haggadah: Music of the Book," a multimedia performance, was composed by Bosnian musician Merima Ključo, who was inspired by the Haggadah's unbelievable journey. As for the Haggadah itself, at the start of 2012, the museum was unable to pay its staff or heating bills and closed its doors, making viewing of the Haggadah, except for scholars, impossible. Fortunately, since 2015, when the museum opened again—it has been displayed on special occasions.

WASHINGTON HAGGADAH

Finally, we meet the Washington Haggadah, so named because it resides in the Judaica collection of the Library of Congress in Washington, DC. I saw it for myself in 2011 when the Haggadah was spending Passover "away from home" on a reading stand inside a case in the medieval art gallery of the Metropolitan Museum of Art in New York, where it was on loan. We know a good deal about its scribe and illuminator, Joel Feibush ben Simeon. He was born in Cologne, Germany, in the mid-fifteenth century and, following the expulsion of Jews from that city, he moved to Bonn. In an era of persecution, Joel crisscrossed between Germany and northern Italy, where he established an atelier. With opportunities for cultural contacts with both Jews and Christians, Joel drew from a broad range of ideas, motifs, and artistic modes, from the more stylized Germanic influence of his background to the intricate Italian elements he adopted.

Joel completed this Haggadah on January 29, 1478. He cleverly introduced himself toward the end of this Haggadah in a colophon by referencing Exodus 36:7: "their efforts had been completed and were more than enough."[21] The passage refers to the Israelites who had been so overwhelmingly generous in their contributions toward the building of the sanctuary that the chief designer of the sanctuary, Bezalel, and his artisans had to turn to Moses to halt the deluge. Perhaps the quote was Joel's way of expressing how challenging his work was. Printing had been invented only two decades before, and the first printed Haggadah had been made just four years previously in Guadalajara, Spain. Joel had to create this Haggadah without a commission already in hand; we know this from the blank pages and margins he left for customization.

Joel introduced lightheartedness, social satire, and ironic tweaks of comic-strip-like humor into the Haggadah. He seized the openings to engage with the Passover story and its interpretations and chronicled holiday preparations woven into the messiness of daily life. He gives a matzah not to the seder leader or guests but to a cartoon-like monkey sitting atop a pillow who plays the matzah as a tambourine. Joel's impish images provided social commentary, as seen in three frequently reproduced pages that tell a story of Italian Jewish domestic life in his time. One image of food preparation features a miserable goitrous fellow in a scruffy tunic who sits on a stool turning the spit as a generous rack of lamb roasts over hot red coals. At the same time, he chugs down a cup of wine and is within easy reach of an ample flask for refills. To his left are two well-dressed Jewish women standing over the pot of soup, stirring. Their dog, eager for a splatter, is underfoot. One woman offers soup to the needy-looking man, not just to feed him but to get him to sober up and concentrate on his task, as if to say in frustration, "Why must women do all the hard work? Enough already!" It is, after all, on the page for "Dayenu," the prayer enumerating God's gifts through history, which concludes after each verse: "It would have been enough!" A woman viewing the image at her own seder may have taken it as her cue that it was time to leave the table (if she ever sat down in the first place) and prepare to serve the meal.

The whimsical commentary on gender continues in a second image. An extremely tall husband tries to stuff a bouquet of bitter herbs into his little wife's mouth, as if to say that she is the source of bitterness in his life. It's a lame joke that other Haggadah artists have used. But Joel introduces a twist: he lets the wife hold her own. Steadied by the double-edged sword she holds, she symbolically resists critique and upholds her integrity.

FIGURE 2.2. Washington Haggadah.

The gendered strife appears somewhat resolved in a third image. A donkey gallops into a doorway of a medieval home, (figure 2.2) welcomed by a husband who has opened up his door at the correct moment in the seder to greet the prophet Elijah—or maybe the Messiah himself—who rides the donkey. Elijah appears to hold a glass of wine in hand, the very one that becomes known as Elijah's Cup in the late medieval period. Behind Elijah sit the passengers: the womenfolk and children, with just enough room remaining at the tail's end for a servant. (In future depictions of Elijah in later editions of the Haggadah, the prophet avails himself of more reliable modes of transportation. In a 1908 Baghdad edition, he arrives by steam engine.) In Joel's fifteenth-century edition, the toast of the husband appears to be reciprocated by his wife, perhaps settling the bickering. The text that accompanies this marginal image provides further venting opportunity for the powerless who cannot, themselves, seek revenge: "Pour out Your wrath upon the nations who do not know You." The verse, taken from Psalm 79, which we have encountered before, probably entered the Haggadah in eleventh- or twelfth-century France around the time of the First Crusade in 1095. It reflected a wish that one day, if not soon then at least at the end of days, God would reenter history and punish all those who caused the Jews to suffer.[22] In the middle ages, there was concern that including the passage would have ramifications, given Christian suspicions about what actually went on in the homes of Jews during seders. The sixteenth-century commentator Eliezer ben Elijah Ashkenazi also worried that the Gentiles among whom they lived would have concluded the Jews were cursing them.

Joel included a hare hunt as a whimsical touch. It comes as a visual pun on the phrase *jag den Häs*, the medieval German term for "hunt the hare." It sounds similar to *YakNeHaZ*, the Talmudic mnemonic for the correct order of rituals and blessings that must be added when the Passover seder occasionally falls on a Saturday night, that is, at sabbath's end, when special blessings are recited. What makes it funny is that the Jewish rules for the proper way to slaughter animals exclude hunted animals; and even if one could eat an animal that was killed by hunters, hares are forbidden. (That said, illustrations of rabbits have continued to race across Haggadot.)

After its creation, the Washington Haggadah wandered along with the Jews who possessed it. There were years in Germany in the sixteenth and seventeenth centuries, and by the nineteenth century, it was being used on Passover by the Provencali family in Mantua, Italy. At the turn of the twentieth century, it was purchased in Italy by Ephraim Deinard, the oversized personality who was a book dealer, bibliographer, polemicist, and parodist. Deinard tried unsuccessfully to sell it for $500 in 1902. Eventually he sold it to the Library of Congress, which added the Haggadah to its collection of nearly 20,000 Hebrew manuscripts. The Library of Congress burnished this Haggadah's public face in 1991 when they published a facsimile with a companion volume by renowned scholars of the day. It was deluxe in every sense of the term: leather bound on vellum, a gilt-lettered custom clamshell box. It was promoted as the perfect gift for the connoisseur, a coffee-table book, not meant for use at the seder table.

In the twenty-first century, the Washington Haggadah became known to a broader public when Harvard University Press issued, as their promotional copy announced: "a stunning facsimile edition meticulously reproduced in full color brings this beautiful illuminated manuscript to a new generation." Affordably priced, unlike the 1991 edition, it came with an accessible scholarly commentary by Haggadah scholars David Stern and Katrin Kogman-Appel. At that time, the Library of Congress digitized the Haggadah, making it viewable from anywhere, at any time. With magnification possible, even the threads tying together the folios are visible!

Having encountered five hundred years of the Haggadah's life as a handmade book, we move to its next incarnation. The technology of printing made available by Johannes Gutenberg and the expanding culture of Hebrew book arts influenced how the Haggadah was produced and transformed. We should note that even after Haggadot began rolling off printing presses, the artisanal production and use of handwritten and illuminated Haggadot has continued. There was a period of revival in the eighteenth century, and to this day, artists are still illuminating Haggadot.

The Printed Haggadah and
Its Enduring Conventions

A Text of One's Own

With the invention of the printing press, the Haggadah became a mass-produced commodity. Manufacturing a Haggadah could be a savvy investment in time and money for a printing house: there was a ready market of Jews worldwide who needed Haggadot for their seders. Nowadays, when scholars and collectors consider early printed Haggadot, they tend to highlight the ones that stand out for their artistry, elegance of printing, influence in their time, and distinguishing features (such as the inclusion of a foldout map) that make them unique or collectible. Those considered particularly significant come from great centers of Hebrew printing and include the Prague edition of 1526, the Mantua editions of 1560 and 1568, several Venice editions printed between 1599 and 1629, and the Amsterdam editions of 1695 and 1712.

Many of the conventions established in the early days of printing endure and are still shaping the Haggadah's contents and appearance. In this chapter, I highlight some of these enduring innovations that came bundled with the new technology.

As a rule, early printed Haggadot were brief. Unadorned ones were as short as twenty pages. With promotional materials, "borrowed" (read: purloined) illustrations, commentary, and instructions, they were no longer than forty pages. Save for costly fine editions created for the well-to-do, printers often economized by using cheap paper, by reusing woodcuts or copperplates until they were worn out, and by making ever-smaller books. When machine-made paper allowed for better-quality affordable copies, families then had the option of replacing Haggadot that had been mishandled, torn, or accidentally drowned in a bowl of saltwater (easy enough to happen with a Haggadah balanced in one hand and a spring green being dipped in saltwater with the other). Growing families needed more copies, and not just for little boys initiated as Hebrew readers, but for women who were depicted in print versions using Haggadot as early as the fifteenth century. Having a Haggadah of one's own to use at the seder—certainly by the nineteenth century—became a signature element of Passover practice. To get an idea of the rapid growth of Haggadah-making since the invention of printing, a trajectory that is clearly in keeping with the general growth of all books, there were twenty-five editions of Haggadot printed in the sixteenth century, thirty-seven in the seventeenth, 234 in the eighteenth, and 1,269 in the nineteenth century.[1]

Perhaps surprisingly, rabbis posed little obstacle to the commercial practices of Hebrew publishing enterprises. They rapidly came around to recognizing how printing expanded the transmission of Jewish learning and, insofar as the Haggadah was concerned, facilitated the observance of Passover at home. In the seventeenth and eighteenth centuries, publishers added authoritative luster to their texts by inviting renowned rabbis to offer letters of approbation (*hashkamot*) to introduce specific Haggadot, a practice that continues to this day.

The very first Haggadah we know of that was printed with moveable type was made by the Soncino family of Guadalajara, Spain, in 1486. It was bound onto a little prayer book, a *sidorello*. The layout and typography are pristine, and while there are no illustrations, there are beautifully designed woodcuts of initial words. The expulsion of Jews from Spain ended the printing of Jewish books there, but Haggadot continued to be printed in Europe, the Ottoman Empire, and North Africa. Despite the burning of Hebrew books and the forcible closings and destruction of presses that printed them; despite laws that forbade Jews from owning presses, thousands of printed Haggadot still managed to emerge and have been preserved.

We'll explore conventions established in the age of printing with an enduring shelf-life by looking primarily at the Amsterdam Haggadah of 1695, whose influence on subsequent printed versions is easily traced.

Jews who had been exiled from Spain and Portugal flourished in Amsterdam, a center of commerce where they could openly practice their faith. Jews were permitted to own their own printing presses, and they produced works of the highest quality, with fine paper and clear type. Unlike the many earlier printed Haggadot that had been illustrated more rustically with woodcuts, the Amsterdam Haggadah was overtly different because it featured a newer printing technique that was already fashionable in the Netherlands: copper engraving. The images created were so much more delicate, precise, and expressive.

Promotional Materials

There is nothing coy or modest about it: the Amsterdam Haggadah unabashedly promotes itself (as well as God's relationship to the Jewish people) on its title page. Readers are greeted with a narrative that parallels the exodus from Egypt and the publication of this particular version of the Haggadah. Its hubris is chatty, with prayer casually tossed in as one might in conversation:

> The Order of the Passover Haggadah, with a pleasant commentary and lovely illustrations of the signs and wonders which the Holy One, blessed be He, performed for our fathers. Added to this are the travels in the wilderness until the division of the Land among the tribes of Israel, and the form of the Temple, may it be restored and rebuilt in our time, Amen. . . . Engraved upon copper tablets by . . . Abraham ben Jacob of the family of Abraham our father. . . . Printed in Amsterdam.[2]

Providing a bountiful amount of information—serving essentially as an advertisement for the book—the narrative intentionally and strategically blurred the distinction between God's miracles and the enticing features of this particular printing. Potential customers perusing this page were alerted to the value of having a "pleasant" commentary (the name of the author, the fifteenth-century Portuguese-born scholar and statesman Isaac Abarbanel [1437–1508][3] is omitted—perhaps because it was so popular that its authorship was taken for granted. The "lovely" illustrations by an artist (who is named) were created using the newer copperplate engraving technique. Images featuring key events in the life of Abraham and his descendants float as medallions above Moses (posing holding the Ten Commandments as horns of light shoot out from behind his head) and his brother Aaron (dressed in the priestly breastplate and swinging the incense he needs for temple sacrifice). They stand, as if on each side of a velvet-curtained stage, as guardians of the historical past and the traditions represented within the very book being held. Moses and Aaron are positioned on the page as orators who proclaim the "copy" placed between them: "How many excellent features the Haggadah includes!" And what better duo than these biblical brothers to endorse the publication? (They might also be stand-ins for Asher Anshel ben Eliezer Chazan and Issacher Ber ben Abraham Eliezer who published this edition at the press of Moses Wiesel.) With no extra cost, the Haggadah offers God's complete collection of signs and wonders. And more—the opening page alludes to the fact that this particular edition comes with a free special bonus: the first ever Hebrew foldout map of the land of Israel in biblical times, including a visual demonstration of the Israelite's successful journey out of Egypt. Many an extant version of this edition is missing its map, suggesting that its owner saw fit to detach the "free gift" and hang it up in their homes for year-round edification and decoration.

I have a theory (indulge me; it's a stretch) about how the curious practice of attaching promotional material coexists readily and comfortably within the pages of printed Haggadot. Here goes: The marriage between advertising and sacred texts did not deviate from Jewish practice; it was a logical outgrowth. Consider this prayer, recited daily, declaring that all of God's powers must be *made known*: "Sing to the Lord all the earth; proclaim His victory day after day. Tell of His glory among the nations, His wondrous deeds among all peoples."[4] Registering gratitude to God quietly to oneself is insufficient; one must repeatedly broadcast it in the form of prayers of praise. When the Passover observance moved from Temple to home, the rabbis said that this new practice counted for fulfilling the imperative to celebrate the historical, miraculous deed of God's rescue of the Jews from bondage in Egypt. The seder effectively "publicized" the miracle. All of the table rituals—drinking the four cups, having a pillow to lean on, and eating matzah—constituted, so to speak, Passover's new advertising campaign. Even the poor were urged to draw money from the community charity so they, too, could have proper seders and be counted among the nation of Passover seder-publicists. Passover influenced the way the rabbis framed the later miracle of Hanukkah, the postbiblical holiday in which publicity, and not just remembrance, was ordained. This is why the lit Hanukkah menorah was initially placed outside one's home (that's still practiced in Israel) so it could be easily seen and its message be read, functioning as a proto-billboard. With publicity as part of the Passover's raison d'être, how easy it was to blur the distinction between the Jew who promoted God and printers who trumpeted the indispensable Haggadah that facilitated the deed. As I said, a theory, but one that would play forward in print Haggadot in America, where promotion extended

72   CHAPTER 3

beyond just the cover page. Companies used the front, back, and inside pages of the Haggadah to advertise products and services a Jewish family might need to observe Passover, say sugar or Breakstone's butter for baking, or a bank to help save year-round for Passover's added expenses. Of course, there is Maxwell House coffee, which created its very own Haggadah, which we will turn to soon.

Haggadah advertising in the form of sponsorship by an individual or a company flourished from the start of the twentieth century. My favorite example, from 1910, is sponsored by quite a character, none other than the clairvoyant and self-declared "Professor" of the Lower East Side, Abraham Hochman. The proprietor of a wedding hall on Sheriff Street called "the headquarters of Love," Hochman described himself as a palm reader, dream interpreter, finder of missing husbands, and advisor on romance and marriage. The cover of the Haggadah with Hochman's name boasted about him and about the Haggadah's additional contents and characteristics as if they were remarkable and not standard fare by that time. These "specials" that were hardly so special included The Song of Songs (recited by many at the seder's end), large print, and instructions in "pure Yiddish" for the rituals, so that "everybody can read and understand."

The free-for-a purchase Maxwell House (or "the traditional Maxwell House" as it is often described with self-mocking affection), still a supermarket favorite, was first published by the Joseph Jacobs Advertising Agency of New York City in the 1920s. Jacobs wanted to market Maxwell House coffee to Jews for their Passover use after he secured rabbinic assurance that coffee beans, which are seeds and not legumes, were indeed permitted for consumption on

Passover. The initial marketing campaign in the Jewish press was persuasive, and Jews learned they could serve the Maxwell House coffee they fancied year-round at their seders. The next step was distributing Haggadot with advertisements for the "good to the last drop" coffee. They were free with purchase of Maxwell House coffee, which explains why people still have so many of them, going back years. The same agency still producing them today claims that to this day, "50 million of these Passover guides have been printed and given away."[5] In advertising lingo that's a "branded utility," a free and useful commodity created by a sponsor for consumers in order to foster relationship, reliance, and confidence. How many other sacred texts could tolerate being branded by a product, by corporate sponsorship? Would we tolerate, much less embrace, a Kleenex Lamentations, or the Lens-Crafters Book of Mormon? Could another sacred text come with tear-out inserts: shopping checklists and advertisements for farfel, gefilte fish balls, macaroons, and candied, jellied slices of "fruit"? Surely, Leviticus could not withstand a centerfold of coupons for an ox of the sacrifice of well-being; the goat for the people's sin offering; 20 percent off turtle-doves and frankincense, two-for-one on pigeons. The aura of the Haggadah proved itself so robust that it apparently resists being diminished by commercial accoutrements.

Affection for this corporate edition was affirmed when news reports of the first ever White House seder revealed that President Barack Obama and his seder mates had selected the "traditional" Maxwell House. It was retranslated in English in 2011 to make it modern-sounding and inclusive (the work was done by a retired Orthodox teacher who confessed he would not use it at his own seder). God is no

longer "He" but "You," the King of the Universe is now a
monarch, and the Four Sons are now children. While the
translation still referred to the "God of our Fathers," God is
no longer described as king, but as a gender-neutral monarch. Still, despite these changes, despite the little girl who
is pictured asking the four questions, the current CEO of
the Joseph Jacobs Advertising Agency made a point of an-
nouncing that this was not a feminist Haggadah; perhaps,
lest it lose its traditional base of consumers. Certainly its
transliterations into the older European Ashkenazi pro-
nunciation of Hebrew that were maintained (perhaps inadvertently?), reminding some baby boomers of Hebrew
School days when they were drilled to ask the Four Questions in this way: *Ma nish-ta-naw ha-lai-law ha-zeh mee-
kawl ha-lay-los?*[6]

BORROWED IMAGES

Let us return to conventions instituted in the printed Amsterdam Haggadah. We see the practice of using—and then
reusing—borrowed images. Its illustrator, Abraham Hakohen, a former pastor and convert to Judaism, borrowed
some images from previous Venetian Haggadot and also
adapted others from the Christian Bible illustrations of
Mattheus Merian of Basel. (Actually, Merian would have
had a hard time claiming infringement of his intellectual
property, as the images he had used were inspired by the
work of Hans Holbein.) Borrowing was typical in printed
Haggadot; what makes Hakohen stand out is his failure to
disguise the Christian content in his images. In one scene

depicting Jerusalem in the messianic era, a little cross atop a tower—oops—has slipped in. Other borrowed images just make only partial sense: Hakohen's wise child, for instance, is a cribbed Hannibal, the general of Carthage; the wicked child is a Roman soldier; the simple child is a young King Saul; and the child who does not know how to ask also happens to be Hannibal (figure 3.1). If the frequent repetition of reproductions of problematic images is any indication, such borrowed images (if they were even noticed) did not arouse concern among readers, and some (in particular, those portraying the wicked son as a non-Jewish soldier) served as models for generations to come.

Hakohen was hardly the only borrower. In the printing industry, used wooden blocks and copper plates were as "movable" as type, and Haggadah images were pirated and freely repurposed for Haggadot and other books as well. Consider a 1606 Venetian commentary on the book of Esther, the text read on the holiday of Purim. Hopefully readers did not look too closely at the image of the holiday feast that was depicted. Had they done so, they would have seen that those were not *hamentashen* (Purim pastries) set out on the table for a Purim feast, but Passover matzahs! The block-printed image of a seder meal was borrowed from a Haggadah from Mantua (1560), which, in turn, had been borrowed from an earlier image in the Prague Haggadah (1527).[7] Queen Esther, in the Venetian edition, is not even really Queen Esther! A close look reveals that she is a repurposed angel of death taken from a Haggadah; she is en route to serve as God's agent in the tenth plague, smiting the firstborn sons of the Egyptians. What then is Esther—who, in the book of Esther, neither flies nor fences—doing with

FIGURE 3.1. Amsterdam Haggadah, 1695.

wings and a sword? Nothing much at all (unless she is contemplating a future as Gal Gadot, the Jewish Israeli actress who plays Wonder Woman).

In the seventeenth and eighteenth centuries, interest in illuminated Haggadot was revived, and in them we see the

The Printed Haggadah and Its Enduring Conventions 77

FIGURE 3.2. Second Cincinnati Haggadah.

continued influence of borrowing practices established earlier. Borrowings from Christian sources are particularly apparent in the 1716 edition of the illuminated Haggadah now referred to as the Second Cincinnati. When Moshe Leib ben Volf of Trebitsch, Moravia, created oil paintings for this edition, he based them on engravings of a version printed in Amsterdam just four years before. Its genealogy went farther back: to our Amsterdam Haggadah of 1695, which, in turn, took inspiration from the King James Bible of 1611.

The convention of freely borrowing the Haggadah's constituent elements remains well and alive to this day. When families (my own included), synagogues, Jewish community groups, and even Christian groups make their own homemade and unpublished Haggadot for their Passover seder, they tend to lift texts and select images from any Haggadah that they like, arrange and edit them (often adjusting them to the attention span of their seder guests), and add their own. Only rarely are attributions ever made in Haggadot created for private use, and when they are, they are usually acknowledged in a general way for their inspiration. Jonathan Safran Foer (whose own published Haggadah inadvertently failed to attribute authorship to a 1982 text of the Rabbinical Assembly) recalled the free access and no attribution approach practiced in his own family: "At each setting was a Haggadah that my parents had assembled by photocopying favorite passages from other Haggadot and, when the Foer finally got Internet access, by printing online sources." Foer coined a marvelous maxim that justified assuming that anything Haggadah related is in the public domain: "Why is this night different from all others? Because on this night copyright doesn't apply."[8]

COMMENTARIES

In the late fifteenth century, the Italian publisher Soncino Press, the first to print the Talmud as a central block of text

FIGURE 3.3. Amsterdam Haggadah, 1695.

surrounded by commentary in smaller type, used a similar
design format for displaying commentary in its Haggadah.
Most Haggadah printings eventually followed this format
in which the Haggadah text was printed in a larger, square-
shaped font, and the one or more commentaries wrapped

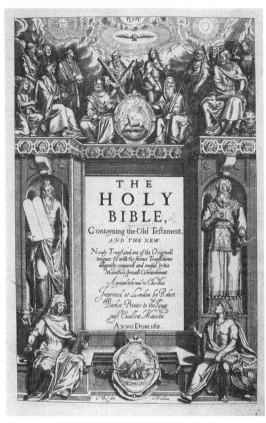

FIGURE 3.4. King James Bible, 1611.

outside it were printed in a smaller, round-shaped font.
Printed Haggadot appeared with diverse and sometimes
multiple commentaries by rabbinic sages, during their life-
times and posthumously. The ever-expanding body of commentaries included those of the Ari (Isaac Luria Ashkenazi,

sixteenth century); Leon of Modena (seventeenth century); the Maharal of Prague (Judah Loew ben Bezalel, sixteenth to seventeenth centuries); Chida (Haim Yosef David Azulai, eighteenth century); and the Vilna Gaon (Elijah Ben Solomon, eighteenth century). Commentaries interpreted the text's meanings, offered theological reflection, and clarified proper observance. They kept the core text relevant and lively with the possibility of continuing thoughtful engagement. They also created a place for authorship in a text that had often been redacted to erase the traces of individual composition.

The Amsterdam Haggadah of 1695 provided commentary in its margins by Don Isaac Abarbanel titled *Zevach Pesach* (Passover Sacrifice) as well as a briefer anonymous mystical commentary at the bottom margin. *Zevach Pesach*, written in Monopli, Italy, in 1496 and first printed in Constantinople in 1505, became one of the most popular commentaries of its century.[9] Abarbanel's questions, one hundred in total, challenged the Haggadah's word choices, contents, and structure. Had the questions not been written by a scholar, statesman, courtier, and leader in the cycle of exile and dispersion as revered as he, one might have thought that a cheeky wicked son had posed them. Here are just three of his challenges. The first concerns word choice: "Why is matzah called poor bread? It is no less tasty or poorer in quality than leavened bread." A second concerns content: "The Four Questions discuss the departures from normal mealtime practices at the seder, such as eating matzah and maror, dipping twice, and reclining. Why is there no mention of other deviations from the norm, such as eating the paschal lamb, drinking the four cups of wine, and washing the hands twice?" A third concerns structure: "Why aren't the four sons arranged in a symmetric fashion, with a fool to offset the wise son, or a saint to counter the evil one? As it is, there is no balance."[10] One can imagine Abarbanel's sharp and pithy questions emboldening seder participants to formulate their own questions without fear of rebuke. His answers, while satisfying, were sermonic, learned, and long, even without the full citations of the biblical proof texts that he referenced.

When Venetian Rabbi Leon of Modena was commissioned to provide a Haggadah commentary appealing to young and old alike for the illustrated 1629 Venice Haggadah, he selected Abarbanel's over his own earlier one. Leon condensed Abarbanel's and called the result *Tzli Esh*, meaning "roasted in fire." The clever title playfully alluded to the passage in Exodus claiming that even after the paschal sacrifice was roasted and shrank, its essence remained fully tasty. By analogy, Modena boasted that his abridged version was as good as, if not better than, Abarbanel's original.

The tradition of providing new and timelier commentaries continues to this day. Publishers often offer Haggadot with the teachings of respected rabbis and teachers, including the Lubavitcher Rebbe, Rabbi Menachem M. Kasher, Rabbi Joseph Soloveitchik, Nechama Leibowitz, Rabbi David Silber, and Rabbi Jonathan Sacks. In 2003, commentaries by dozens of Jewish women, rabbis, and scholars were presented in two volumes, "The Woman's Passover Companion," and "The Woman's Seder Sourcebook" (these were an outgrowth of a tradition of women's seders at Yale University). An ambitious contemporary pair of volumes, *My People's*

Passover Haggadah appeared in 2008, providing extensive commentaries from eleven rabbis and scholars drawn from multiple denominations and representing perspectives including theology, history, Hasidism, Jewish law, and feminism.

Translations

Although Jerusalem remained the spiritual center of Judaism, there have been many living centers of Jewry, even if they lasted only for a time. Wherever they settled, Jews absorbed the languages of these places, and print Haggadot reflected this. The Venice Haggadah of 1609 provided three columns of translation featuring Judeo-Italian, Judeo-German (Yiddish), and Judeo-Spanish (Ladino). Our Amsterdam Haggadah of 1695 appealed to both Sephardi and Ashkenazi Jews, with instructions appearing in Ladino and Yiddish; the seder signs were also translated into Judeo-Italian. A multilingual format offered spatial representation of the unity of a people, even though dispersed and diverse in practice. (One might ask if readers were distracted by having to ignore the presence of alternative languages and ritual choices. I suspect this was not a problem for the learned in particular, who were used to consulting pages of printed sacred text that held more sources of commentary than they could possibly consult at a single encounter.) By the seventeenth century, complete bilingual translations of the Haggadah were printed in European languages, with Spanish as the first.

The Amsterdam Haggadah, providing multiple vernacular languages (and options for Sephardic and Ashkenazic rites as well), set a standard of accessibility for Haggadot produced for Jews wherever they lived, including those who lived in places considered far-flung. Earlier, I mentioned the Haggadah translated into Marathi for the indigenous Bene Israel of India. This 1846 Haggadah was created with a "missionizing" goal, so to speak. While honoring the particularity of this isolated group, it also encouraged their conformity to the "normative" rabbinic practices followed by Jews of Cochin and Baghdad. In a 1874 Poona edition printed with a Marathi translation, lithographs depict women wearing saris and flowers in their hair and men wearing tunics as they squat or kneel on the floor, busily going through the steps of shaping and baking matzahs.

In our time, the 2012 Haggadah for and about Ethiopian Jews, "The Koren Ethiopian Haggada: Journey to Freedom," displays a similar two-pronged strategy of providing accessibility while simultaneously pushing for conformity. On the one hand, it expresses concern for Ethiopian Jews who have found refuge in Israel and respects the particularity of their history. In text and photographs, this Haggadah tells the story of the Beta Yisrael (the community's preferred name for itself), recounting its hardships, rescue, and complicated resettlement in Israel. It documents distinctive ways they observe Passover and acknowledges that immigration to Israel has taken a toll on the community's practices and authority of its rabbis. On the other hand, it quietly downplays their community's ritual and liturgical differences (in particular, the absence in Ethiopia of a set written text[11]) and appears to encourage assimilation. It seems to me that it does this by featuring the text and order of the seder of Sephardic Israelis, implying that this is the model to which Ethiopians must conform in order to "adapt to life in the Land of Israel."[12]

Historically speaking, not all translations of printed Haggadot were up to par, especially when the editing was sloppy. This we learn from an emerging Passover practice, the publication of the Haggadah review. In his 1890 column in the *Jewish Standard* called "Morour and Charouseth," the British humorist Israel Zangwill pilloried an English-Hebrew Haggadah published in Vienna in 1886: "If there is any good English version of the Haggadah, it has never been my good fortune to come across it. Each year I seem to get hold of an edition which is funnier than the previous year's." Among the blunders Zangwill selected are these gems: "Jacob wrestled with a mangle," "The day draws night," "we are duty bound to . . . bless, exalt and reference him," "the bread of afflication," and "They have hands but teel not." He pleaded: couldn't some publisher bring out a proper English edition?

EXPLANATIONS

Early on, publishers of printed Haggadot determined their householder-customers could use easy-to-understand and practical explanations of the rituals and their significance. So the books offered verbal and visual prompts for preparing a home for Passover and instructions for making one's way through the lengthy and complex seder. The Amsterdam's explanations are mostly brief and to the point: say this blessing when Passover begins on the sabbath . . . say that blessing and fill the second cup. In later printed Haggadot, the explanatory materials grew more extensive. Consider these explanatory notes accompanying the bilingual edition of a Haggadah translated into English by the printer A. Alexander, which first appeared in London in 1770 in Ashkenazic and Sephardic editions. This Haggadah contains, as its title page announces:

CEREMONIES and PRAYERS
Which are ufed and read
By all FAMILIES, in all Houses
of the
I S R A E L I T E S
THE
Two Firft Nights of PASSOVER:
Faithfully TRANSLATED from the
ORIGINAL HEBREW
TO WHICH IS ADDED,
The EXPLANATION thereon.[13]

Most of Alexander's explanations were meant to be read before the seder, in preparation. From the topics raised, we can glimpse practices common in the London of Alexander's time and issues that might have perplexed householders, male and female alike. Could additional wine be served with the meal? How did you re-create a lounge chair for the master of the house? How were you supposed to treat your Jewish servants during the seder? And what was the right way to dispose of Elijah's cup of wine after he has "visited"? On these matters, Alexander advised:

. . . every person at the Table has his glass or cup filled with wine, at this ceremony four different times . . .

though at supper many more are made use of, but at the ceremony no more than four.

The seat of the master is three chairs close together, in imitation of a couch, at the head of which, are put pillows to raise it high, for the master to lean on while he sets at table.

In all families, the meanest of the Hebrew Servants are seated at table, these two nights with their masters and mistresses, and the rest of their superiors.

One cup of wine is always set on the table extraordinary for Elias [*sic*] the Prophet to drink of (which is drank by the youngest at the Table, in his stead), and filled with the rest.[14]

What about the three matzahs displayed in a pile on the table; what do they mean? Print Haggadot offered multiple interpretations of what they and the broken middle matzah symbolized. In the Prague Haggadah of 1526 (noted for its beauty and use of multiple fonts), the three matzahs reference the three types of bread the ancient priests sacrificed in the temple. According to the 1869 Parisian Haggadah (intended for Jews observing German and Portuguese rites), the matzahs symbolized different levels of Jewish ancestry, a popular explanation. The bottom matzah represented the ordinary Israelites and the middle and top layer matzahs stood for the priestly classes of Temple days: the Kohanim and the Levites. If we jump ahead to the 2008 Haggadah of Jonathan Sacks, then chief rabbi of the United Kingdom, we see the relevance of this ritual given a psychological twist, evocative of our era's concerns. The broken matzah represents both freedom and slavery. "The difference between freedom and slavery," Sacks explains, "does not lie in the quality of the bread we eat, but the state of mind in which we eat it."[15]

Haggadot of the earlier centuries of the printed era established conventions that became, in time, new traditions. Particular reinventions of the Haggadah created and printed in America and Israel pointedly broke with tradition and then established new conventions whose influence continues to reverberate. It is to these Haggadot, new members of the family tree, that we turn to now.

Twentieth-Century Variations

The Haggadah in American Jewish Movements,
Israeli Kibbutzim, and American Third Seders

In the previous phase of the Haggadah's life, its text had become largely set, and when its meanings were expanded, it was through the reframing of commentary and art. Haggadah reshapers of the twentieth century saw fit to change the text itself. In this chapter, we look at three distinct contexts for innovation.

When the liberal Reform movement took hold, first in Europe and then in America, its new breed of rabbis, trained in the scientific and historical study of textual traditions, created Haggadot reflecting models of being Jewish in line with Jewish ideologies. These Haggadot, however different, shared much in common with those developed by pioneers of kibbutzim, cooperative agricultural settlements established in Palestine on lands that became part of the State of Israel after 1948. Further, these two sources of new Haggadot, Reform and kibbutzim, shared much in common with secular Yiddish *hagodes*, composed by Jewish socialist revolutionaries from Eastern Europe, and widely used in the first half of the twentieth century in America by Yiddish-speaking immigrants and their families in celebrating a new American tradition—an alternative third seder.

What could these three distinctive sources of Haggadot, meant for such different communities, have in common, making them relatives of a fashion? They shared these traits: While challenging the authority of traditional Judaism, they took it for granted that Passover was a Jewish holiday of supreme importance for Jews, and the Haggadah was its medium for Jewish transmission. Still, all sought a break with the ancestral Haggadah and overcame any nostalgia for it in order to make a radical departure. All believed they were free to reject the rituals stipulated by Jewish law in order to reinterpret them. If sections of the Haggadah were deemed to be no longer relevant, they could be altered, rejected, and even, in later years, revived. In all three contexts, the Haggadah was—as it has been since its conception—a site for negotiation. It provided the platform for reframing the meanings of former Jewish practices, promoting new ones, and trying out new theologies. For Reform Jews, it provided a platform for decorous worship and the embrace of America as a New Jerusalem. For both kibbutz members and the observers of the third seder, the Haggadah affirmed the meaningfulness of a Judaism in which God was largely absent. Within their particular contexts, these new Haggadot recontextualized the traditional Passover narrative by interpreting the relationship between the Jewish past and the present they inhabited.

Did the new variants of the Haggadah introducing texts and practices destroy the Passover practices of Jewry worldwide? Hardly. Distinctive local and household customs had long colored how Jews across the world conducted their seders. (Not all those accumulated practices were written down in Haggadot, some were preserved orally as *min-hag*, treasured tradition.) Jews of Persia and Afghanistan whacked each other (playfully) during *Dayenu* with scallions, recalling the Egyptian taskmasters' whips and the Israelites' desires for a tastier menu than manna during their desert wanderings. Moroccan Jews passed the seder plate over the head of each guest, reciting, "In haste, we went out of Egypt with our bread of affliction and now we are free." Hungarian Jews decorated their seder table with gold and silver jewelry in remembrance of the passage in Exodus in which Egyptians gave the freed Israelites gold and silver. Egyptian and Syrian Jews wrapped the matzah in a sack, passing it from person to person, asking and answering each time, in Arabic,

"Where are you coming from?"
"From Egypt."
"What are you carrying?"
"Matzot."
"Where are you going?"
"To Jerusalem."

Many of these customs are still practiced in their communities of origin; some have been borrowed by those seeking novelty to spice up dull seders.

The meaning of exile and homeland shifted in these three twentieth-century variations on the Haggadah. Reform Jews in America, particularly immigrants and their children, celebrated a Jewish-infused version of democracy. Although the age-old reference to the Haggadah's concluding refrain,

"Next year in Jerusalem," still represented a symbolic wish for Jewish unity, well-being, and peace, many of the early generations of American Reform Jewry had little desire to be delivered by God to the land of the Bible. The founding members of the kibbutz movement, for their part, had refused to wait passively for a messiah to lead them back from exile to the Promised Land. They achieved it themselves by training in agriculture, packing their bags, leaving their families, and making their way to Ottoman Palestine on their own. "Next year in Jerusalem" was neither a hope nor a dream for them, but rather the ground they were establishing. As for the secular Jews at third seders, the inclusion of Israel in their Haggadot promoted their particular organizations' range of stances toward Zionism.

All of these new Haggadot were works in progress, fluid scripts tried out on the children and adults who performed them. From extant volumes, editor's notes, archived proceedings, memoirs, and histories, we can trace how subsequent editions in each category provided further chances to keep on revising.

Reform Haggadot

The first English-language Haggadah of the British Reform movement was printed in England in 1842. This was Reverend David Woolf Marks's Haggadah Lepesach: *Domestic Service for the First Night of Passover*.[1] With an eye toward clarity, brevity, and decorum, Marks privileged the biblical passages and interpretive readings over the traditional ceremony. He added clarifying readings from Exodus and decreased the ceremonial drinking of wine. Four cups of wine were reduced to one, perhaps expressing the movement's aspiration for respectability?

The Reform movement's 1907 Union Haggadah, made in America, came about in response to an urgent 1904 report of the three rabbinic members of its Committee on the Pesach Haggadah. They criticized the traditional text of the Haggadah for being out of touch with the feelings of the modern Jew. They minced no words. It was

> obsolete and tasteless, at times giving offense to our sense of devotion. This is due to the commingling of purely religious elements with the didactic, of inane sophistical discussions with the announcement of lofty precepts, the humorous with the tragic, psalms with jingling rhymes, universal truths with narrow materialistic concepts.[2]

The dated artwork of printed Haggadot, the "quaint and grotesque efforts" of early artists whose work has "continued to be reproduced with dreary monotony," needed to go, too: "Too long have we been satisfied with the dry husks of medievalism."[3] For the sake of solidarity among Reform Jews, they urged for a standard and tasteful seder service, a new Haggadah embodying the quaint charms of the original, provided it could reflect the spirit of the day.

A sole member of the committee, Rabbi Barnett A. Elzas of Charleston, South Carolina, opposed "any modern Haggadic hotch-potch" and would have been satisfied with keeping "*all* the old . . . (and) cutting out what is objectionable and substituting where necessary."[4] Nonetheless, a new Haggadah was prepared for the enlightened "modern man" whose sensitivities were said to be irritated by rituals that were "vested . . . with mystic meaning, or supernatural sanction." This modern man did not see rituals as obligations commanded by God but as "potent object lessons of great events and of sublime principles hallowed and intensified in meaning by ages of devout usage."[5]

Out went the four questions. One succinct two-part question for the youngest to ask in both Hebrew and English sufficed: "Why is this night distinguished from all other nights and what is the meaning of this service?" The novel question merited a novel response: Jews gathered on this night to recall that God delivered their ancestors from Egypt, and as a consequence, they were bound to announce monotheism and deliver humankind. God was praised for dispensing this noble, ethical, and universal task.

More familiar elements were excised. Out went the drops of wine on the seder plate that evoked the ten plagues of the Exodus story. Out went the "inane sophistical discussions"—that is, the hard-to-follow midrash of the ancient rabbis. Out went the phrase "Next year in Jerusalem."

In lieu of yearning for an end of exile came a wish for the wrongs of the past to be righted with the coming year. Materials deemed supplementary were relegated to an appendix of descriptions of the history of Passover and its practices. Given that a minimum of Hebrew was included, the book was oriented from left to right, in the manner of English books. Traditional elements judged to lend color to the service were permitted to remain, including the "living words of instruction" (that is, many biblical passages) and acceptable "ceremonial acts" that stimulated the sentiment of "warm religious sympathy" between parent and child. Characteristic of the era, the Haggadah valued the domestic charm of a family singing accompanied by piano (permitted on the holiday for Reform Jews). Consequently, it provided musical notation for prayers and songs in English and Hebrew.

The Union Haggadah saluted the pride and gratitude Jews felt for their freedom as American citizens by celebrating "the brave parts taken by Jews in the struggles of the nations which they have become identified."[6] (This was a sentiment expressed in earlier progressive American Haggadot, such as one by Rabbi Morris Jastrow, who mused in 1891 on "what duties are incumbent upon the Israelite of our own days, and especially in countries like ours, where the morn of religious liberty has already dawned and is shedding its roseate light over all inhabitants alike."[7]) To stress its American orientation, the Union Haggadah included a photograph of the 1876 sculpture *Religious Liberty* (installed in Philadelphia) celebrating American independence by Moses Ezekiel. As the first Jew to attend the Virginia Military Institute and as a soldier in the Confederate Army who defended Richmond, Ezekiel exemplified loyal American citizenship. (Given the editors' artistic ambitions for their text, one might have thought they would have included more bold images. But there were only pen-and-ink decorations, a reproduction of a seder dish, and one of Moritz Oppenheim's 1837 oft-reproduced sentimental painting called *Seder Eve*—literally Der Oster-Abend, Easter Eve—depicting a bourgeois German family including three sons and a daughter, all at their places at the table, Haggadot in hand.)

A 1923 revision of the Union Haggadah brought back more Hebrew and introduced "musical numbers" such as "America." Even more different in both perspective and content was the Reform movement's 1974 edition. Reform Jews were embracing once-scorned traditional liturgies and practices and were rejecting the hyper-rationalism of the earlier versions. With Leonard Baskin's elegant and colorful watercolors, alternately moody and decorative, and with relevant selections from the writings of Anne Frank, Albert Einstein, Elie Wiesel, Martin Buber, and Hayim Nachman Bialik, this version was immediately popular, and it remained so, with over a million copies sold. Editing the new work, Herbert Bronstein wrote: "this Haggadah is not a revision of the previous Union Haggadah. It is an attempt at *renovatio ab origine*: a return to the creative beginning so as to bring forth what is utterly new from what was present in the old."[8]

Even more Hebrew was included. Restored were the ten plagues, though they were preceded by a litany of traditional apologetics, such as the Talmudic passage in which God silences the angels who rejoice as the Egyptians drown by telling them, "My creatures are perishing and you sing praises?"[9] At that juncture, seder participants were to recite a passage identifying them as a dignified people who take no pleasure in revenge:

> Though we descend from those redeemed from brutal
>   Egypt,
> and have ourselves rejoiced to see oppressors overcome,
> yet our triumph is diminished
> by the slaughter of the foe,
> as the wine within the cup of joy is lessened
> when we pour ten drops upon Egypt.[10]

Restored, too, was the wish for a next year in Jerusalem, though longing for a homeland was expressed as an expansive wish for world peace and universal freedom, a spiritual journey from darkness to collective light. This was a mystical Jerusalem where all people will come together; Zion was now a place of "love and peace,"[11] a turn of phrase reflecting its 1970s composition.

Interestingly, in 2014, the Reform movement, having noted that the 1923 version continues to be dear to a segment of its members, issued a New Union Haggadah, which visually resembles the 1923 version, with its art deco images and high-toned poetic text of yesteryear. Look carefully, and it does have updates: gender inclusive language, and two feminist innovations we will discuss later: a cup for Miriam and an orange on the seder plate.

Kibbutz Haggadot

The first kibbutzim were established by idealistic and ideologically driven young Zionists of Eastern Europe, primarily Poland and Russia. Among the hallmarks of this experiment in communal living, begun in 1910, were the dignity of agricultural labor, the rejection of bourgeois culture, and the freedom from constraining religious beliefs and practices of the traditional Judaism of Eastern Europe. Kibbutz members dwelled, dined, and worked together as comrades. Some housed children separate from their parents and raised them cooperatively. They spoke a language under construction, modern Hebrew. They challenged the inherited Jewish view of masculinity. The pious and politically passive Torah scholar beholden to God's will was cast aside in the new Zionist popular imagination. He was replaced by a muscular utopic visionary, bound by shared destiny to his commune. He drove a tractor, safeguarded his community, and built a nation. But would he celebrate Passover and use a Haggadah?

In equipping themselves psychically for nation building, kibbutz members initially objected in principle to rehearsing the collective memory of their ancestors' oppression under Pharaoh. Their redemption did not come from a God whose existence they questioned or repudiated. In their everyday lives, kibbutz members saw themselves as the sources of their own security, the authors of their own freedom, and guarantors of their own passage back to their homeland. Moreover, some kibbutz members found seder observance simply too sad to endure. What was the point of sitting at tables in the communal dining hall symbolically reenacting all this? The sight of the hall prepared for the holiday made them wistful for festive times in their childhood families.

But the holiday and its Haggadah still beckoned, so much so that on the kibbutzim, between 1930 and 1950, some five hundred to a thousand Haggadot were developed. At some kibbutzim, members performed the old text in a perfunctory matter, following an abbreviated seder with zesty singing and dancing of newly invented "folk" dances late into the night. Some parodied the Haggadah, reflecting the strident antireligious attitude of the day. (The comic approach rested on a rich tradition of Jewish satire of sacred texts. The Haggadah, in particular, had frequently been subverted in the past, and especially after the Enlightenment. Yiddish-language socialist parodies of the Haggadah had already appeared in Soviet Russia of the 1920s.[12])

Members of Kibbutz Afikim, located near the Sea of Galilee, once celebrated Passover in a mocking, comic way, with members wearing nightdresses and towels on their heads. The traditional story of the Four Sons lent itself especially well to kibbutz adaptation. Addressing work conditions—and in particular the problem of the lazy comrade—the 1939 Haggadah of Kibbutz Ramat Yochanan provided a section titled "The Kibbutz Bell and the Four Sons." Its wicked son says, "The bell is for you, not for me. And since he removed himself from the group, he transgressed the group's main principle."[13]

These early years of ambivalence or rejection soon passed on secular kibbutzim, and Passover became the central Jewish holiday. Understandably: a newly established nation called for shared celebrations offering opportunities to create collective memories, even as its history was still unfolding. Core values, as they were being negotiated, were transmitted and enforced through collective performance. Passover had become a time for annual meetings, conversations about the future of the kibbutz, and even weddings. In seemingly endless committee meetings, members created alternative Haggadot. They turned what they considered a frozen document into a vital one, producing, reproducing, and distributing collective Jewish identities. There was a change in attitude: "this custom of mockery . . . in which the verses were twisted . . . is stopped," said one member. "Now the custom is to make it a context (*sic*), a puzzle of Torah and prophets chapters, early and late poets and to tell in it the exodus of our fathers as well as our own." Observing that kibbutzim were competing to make their Haggadot even more artistic than those of their neighbors, it was concluded, "there is no bigger joy than the rustle of the unified turning of the page by tens and hundreds of the recliners and the beating of the hearts which follows it."[14]

The Haggadot celebrated the kibbutz's accomplishments, chronicled its history, articulated its ideologies, and marked tragedies and threats. The Haggadot championed Jewish national independence, the settlement of the land, and the welcoming of new waves of immigrants. Stencils made the proliferation of Haggadot in kibbutzim possible. They were typed or hand-lettered and hand-illustrated (and some, hand-painted), then copied onto white or colored paper in small runs on mimeograph machines.[15] Rosters of babies born that year, reports of the year past, and plans for the year to come were included, making annual revisions necessary. Later, as kibbutzim became more established, editors of the major kibbutz federations worked up standard texts for its members and the city folks who flocked to kibbutzim as Passover guests. As the years passed, there were eventually larger print runs, professionally printed and illustrated, and sold to people in the cities and abroad who were fascinated by the kibbutz in the years that it flourished. By that point, while certain hallmarks of kibbutz Haggadot were retained, a return to incorporate more traditional texts was already under way.

From the start, biblical themes linked to nature seemed worthy of reframing for their timeliness. The first was the renewal of springtime: Jews who had arrived from Europe and Russia celebrated the Passovers of their youth in the lingering last days of winter. Now in Palestine, Passover and springtime weather coincided, and it meant something to celebrate the end of the rainy season at this point of the year and to hope for an abundance of dew, in accordance with the liturgy of the prayer book. The seasonal verses of Song of Songs, already read traditionally on Passover, were ripe for plucking: "For the winter is past, the rain is over and gone; The flowers appear on the earth; the time of singing is come, and the voice of the turtle dove is heard in our land" (2:11–12). Illustrations of springtime and joyous signs of renewal filled the pages, as kibbutz artists drew scenes they were actually witnessing: wildflowers, birds in their nests, growing grain, lambs being born. These images shared the page with emergent icons of kibbutz life: cypress trees, watchtowers and water towers, early tents, and implements of agriculture.

Passover was becoming an ever-expanding venue for the artistic creativity of groups and individuals, amateurs and professionals. Long in advance of the holiday, skits were rehearsed, cantatas composed. Hayim Atar, a painter at Kibbutz Ein Harod, covered the walls of the kibbutz dining hall on Passover "with verses, floral patterns and legendary creatures that seem to have been transposed to here from ancient Jewish manuscripts and from paintings of the timber synagogues in Eastern Europe."[16] At Kibbutz Yagur in 1938, Yehuda Sharet composed and directed a Passover eve cantata performed for the assembled members by kibbutz choruses, soloists, and musicians. This model spread to other kibbutzim, solidifying the centrality of musical performance and group song in Passover observance.

The typical secular kibbutz Haggadah featured nature-based themes that were declared through excerpts from the Song of Songs, medieval poetry, and visual images of nature. In lieu of blessing God over four cups of wine, one toasted comrades and children, the fruit of the land, the fruits of collective efforts, and the blessing of life. After 1948, one Haggadah gave each of the four cups a theme: Jewish statehood, worker's freedom, world peace, and the fruits of socialist work. New Four Questions pointed out what was actually taking place in their lives. Why were children not eating separately in their own dining halls, but rather with the whole community? Why was talking of mundane matters replaced by telling the Exodus story? In this version below, we see how events of the day influenced the text. This 1939 Haggadah of Kibbutz Tel Yesef asks how the day is different at a time of Nazi persecution, illegal immigration to Palestine, and fighting with Arabs. In part, the answer:

> On all other days there is both an aspiration for peace and for war in the world. In these days the entire world is moving towards war. . . . During all the years of building the homeland we were acquainted with periods of expansion and of restrictive decrees. In these days they seek to uproot everything.[17]

Shortly after, reflecting World War II in 1942, Kibbutz Naan's Haggadah asked,

> Why is the position of the Jews different from that of all the nations? For every nation dwells in its house and homeland, but the Jews are scattered throughout the world, hated, persecuted, and even to the Land of Israel, their homeland, they are not permitted to come without hindrance?[18]

The parallels between the suffering of Jews under Pharaoh and their current struggles were clearly drawn. The Exodus story itself was relayed with a new emphasis on human agency and personal reckoning. God remained as a character in the story but was no longer the source for faith in a better future. Replacing the rabbinic sages were Hebrew poets and writers including Bialik, Rachel, Shlonsky, and Tchernikowsky. The words of Katzenelson, who lost his wife and son and then perished himself in Auschwitz, appeared in 1947 in the Haggadot of various kibbutzim:

> I dreamed a most terrible dream—
> My people no longer exists, it is no more . . .
> I weep in my anguish by day and by night,
> Why, my Lord, wherefore, O God?[19]

In the Bet Ha-Shitah Haggadah, Katzenelson's poem hovers over the darkness surrounding a grieving man in a fetal position. This image sits in striking juxtaposition with one earlier in the text in which, under bright lights illuminating a kibbutz dining room, many animated Jews assemble to celebrate a seder in joy and safety.

Before days of remembrance were designated in Israel to mourn the Holocaust, grieve for soldiers lost in its wars, and celebrate independence,[20] the work of liturgical marking was done on the pages of kibbutz Haggadot. They incorporated writings, memories, and tributes to the dead, the fallen, survivors, and heroes. Once official national days were established in Israel to mark these events and losses, texts that had entered the Haggadah to express mourning or joy and pride were gradually pared down and incorporated into the appropriate new national ceremonies where they fit more appropriately.

Secular Third Seders

Socialist activists of the Jewish labor movement were among the Jewish immigrants to North America who had migrated to America in the first decades of the twentieth century. Many had left religious Judaism behind in Eastern Europe. Rejecting what they considered its supernaturalism and superstitions, they still kept their pact with Jews as a people and with *yiddishkayt*, the rich Jewish cultural life of the old country. Their language was Yiddish, and in America's big cities, they formed fraternal organizations for mutual aid and organizing. On Passover, they came together at public banquets as proud secular Jews for special or "third seders." For the sake of keeping up social relations, they avoided the first evenings of the seder so that people might attend gatherings with friends and family, and the "third" seder was held during the festival week or just after. The Arbeter Ring (Workmen's Circle), whose Haggadah was called *A naye hagode shel peysakh* (a New Haggadah for Passover), held its first seder in a hall in New York in 1922 for its children being taught to embrace secular Yiddish culture. It grew into an organizational celebration of Passover in Yiddish poetry and political debate. Needing more space for all their members, the seder moved to the ballroom of the Waldorf Astoria hotel, and by 1953, a thousand people attended. The Labor Zionist Alliance, Yiddishists who supported the Zionist option, developed a Haggadah called *Hagode shel paysakh farn dritn seyder* (Haggadah for Passover for the third seder) that included new texts by Yiddish writers of the day. Their seders began modestly in 1927 and grew into gala events, with speakers, professional singers, stars of the Yiddish stage, and celebrities such as Frank Sinatra.

In April 1945, ten thousand Jews came to third seders held by the Jewish Labor Committee for Palestine at both the Astor and Commodore Hotels. There, they raised funds for Israel and listened to a message sent by President Franklin Delano Roosevelt expressing his sympathy for the "unparalleled sufferings" of the Jewish people in the war years.

Similar to kibbutz seders, the various third seders were not held in individual homes but communally, in rented halls. That was the right venue for cultivating group cohesiveness and transmitting the group's ideology, stressing themes of solidarity, freedom, and organizing for the rights of workers. In the case of the Labor Zionists, support for Zionism and the establishment of the State of Israel were central, and fund-raising was part of the evening's program. Could the traditional Haggadah—which had been initially mocked—be mined as a vehicle for this kind of social activism? Back in 1887, in Vilna, the Russian Social Democratic Workers' Party had already developed such editions, as had the Jewish Labor Bund. America's Jewish Labor movement determined they could also use the Haggadah to champion progressive politics. New Haggadot told the Exodus story by stressing the heroism of Moses, revolutionary and champion of human rights who emerged *In dem land fun piramidn* (in the land of the pyramids) and who came, as described in a Yiddish seder song, "[to] free us finally." Symbols on the Passover plate, liberated from divine and rabbinic command, were repurposed as symbols of liberation from political, economic, and religious oppression. In a 1955 English-language version of the Arbeter Ring's Haggadah, the ten plagues were denoted as "aggressive war, communism, fascism, slave labor, genocide, disease, famine, human exploitation, religious bigotry, and racial discrimination." Blessings, such as the one said as candles were lit ("Blessed are you, Lord our God, Ruler of the universe who commands us to light the festival candles") were recast as statements. The poem *Tsint on di likht*, from a Haggadah of the Arbeter Ring, offers this picture of Jewish domestic bless, as a mother freely chooses to set her Passover table and share it lovingly with her child.

> Light the candles from end to end,
> Adorn the table with fresh-smelling flowers.
> Three beautiful roses—bright and fine,
> Pick, my child.
> Dip the morer, karpas, in kharoyses.[21]

AN EXCURSUS: HAGGADOT OF OTHER AMERICAN JEWISH COMMUNITIES

Before we move on, we'll round out our picture of how the Haggadah was shaped in the contemporary era by taking a brief glance at the equally rich and complex Haggadot of other Jewish movements—Reconstructionist, Conservative, and Orthodox—that also flourished in twentieth-century America.

Like the Reform Haggadot, the 1941 Haggadah of the new Reconstructionist movement reframed the traditional one in radical ways, preaching ethical self-betterment and the theme of freedom, particularly at the outset of World

War II. It author, Rabbi Mordecai Kaplan, founder of Judaism's Reconstructionist movement, eliminated many of the rabbinic interpretations in order to provide American families with an engaging and informative retelling of the Exodus story. Kaplan believed that the traditional Haggadah was itself a factor leading to the desuetude of home seders; they had become meaningless and uninspiring. By articulating the biblical story unleashed from its supernatural origins and clearly drawing out its themes of freedom, Kaplan thought his Haggadah could make homes more intensively Jewish and make the seder a "living Jewish experience." Foreshadowing how important social activism would one day become in Haggadot, the New Haggadah featured a social-activist Moses, without fear that he would draw attention away from God as the sole rescuer. The Haggadah was purchased by diverse householders and rabbis who cherished and used it for years, supplementing it by dipping back into their more traditional Haggadot for endearing parts—naming the plagues, in particular—that they missed.

Kaplan's changes, meant to blow off the "sacred dust," precipitated a storm! His then-colleagues at the Jewish Theological Seminary, the rabbinical school of the Conservative movement, saw his innovations as radical acts flying in the face of historical appropriateness (and, not to mention, their own authority). The irate seminary professors, headed by Professor Louis Finkelstein, wrote a group letter dated April 31, 1941:

> The term Haggadah itself is quite a misnomer for your book. It is, if you will, a new Passover service. But a book, which omits *derashah*, or rabbinic interpretation of the

biblical verses, has ceased to be a Haggadah; for the word Haggadah is a technical term, applying to the interpretation of a biblical text.

Originally, it could be taken for granted that Jews knew the bare-bones biblical story by heart. But not in America of 1941. This is one reason why contemporary Haggadot have continued in Kaplan's path, serving up more Bible, either straight up from the book of Exodus, or through skits that can be dramatized. As for Kaplan's hope to create a "living Jewish experience"[22]—as we shall see in chapter 6, the experiential aspect of the Haggadah will widen in ways he could never have imagined.

The Haggadot used and created by the Conservative movement, established at the turn of the twentieth century, had no intention of dismantling Haggadah traditions of the past. Many Conservative Jewish homes used traditional Haggadot with English translations. These included Rabbi Nathan Goldberg's 1949 Haggadah that proved so useful to after-school Hebrew school students and their teachers, and the Haggadah of Rabbi Morris Silverman, liturgist of the Conservative movement. Silverman pointedly included both the American and Israeli national anthems in his edition, affirming that one could feel allegiance to Israel and still be a patriotic American. (To give credit where it is due: it was Lillian Cowan who established in her much revised 1904 Haggadah the convention of incorporating patriotic songs—including *Hatikva*, adopted in 1897 as an anthem by the First Zionist Congress.)

While many Conservative Jews were happy using the Maxwell House Haggadah, the movement's Rabbinical

Assembly decided in the 1970s to produce a Haggadah of its own. After a 1979 prototype was test-run by hundreds of rabbis and congregants who relayed their comments, a forerunner of crowdsourcing, in 1982 *Passover Haggadah: The Feast of Freedom* was released. It reflected the movement's ideology: respect for Jewish law, practice, and scholarship in the light of changing modern realities. So faithful was this Haggadah to the traditional Hebrew text that innovations made to the core text are actually hard to detect, reflecting how adept the editors were in counterbalancing "conservation and innovation."[23] But the spirit of innovation is there. It was also one of the earliest Haggadot edited by a woman, Rachel Anne Rabinowicz, who died at a young age, only years after its publication. The Haggadah offers six pages of text linking the Holocaust to the founding of the State of Israel, affirming the centrality of Israel to Conservative Jews. There were the fresh insights in marginal commentaries by Rabbi Michael Strassfeld, an author of the popular do-it-yourself "Jewish Catalog," and the artwork of Dan Reisinger, a Bezalel-trained Israeli artist and Holocaust survivor. His colorful illustrations, which have the feel of torn paper, are decidedly modern in style. The most frequently reproduced image from this Haggadah is his rendering of the Four Sons. Reisinger created each with composite parts of all three others, a strong visual midrash, showing how aspects of wisdom, challenge, simplicity, and silence are part of each person.

American Jews raised in the Orthodox tradition of the mid-twentieth century frequently used the Birnbaum Haggadah or the Maxwell House, which by the 1960s was considered fully "kosher" by virtue of the involvement of the

Orthodox rabbis and scholars who worked on it. I grew up spending seders at my grandparents' Orthodox home where we happened to use the miniscule Abraham Regelson 1951 Haggadah. How much I inadvertently learned by scrutinizing Siegmund Forst's illustrations! The very happy Jewish boy in a green suit and bow tie who, in the glow of candles, got to read the Four Questions confirmed that God preferred boys over girls. From the lively men and women in shorts who were happily harvesting bananas, I learned that life in Israel seemed much better than in New Jersey. But Israel was also dangerous: the merry farmers were guarded by two more shorts-wearing figures, one a tall heroic type toting a gun and the other a meek, hunched companion, dressed in prayer garb. The preface claimed these new illustrations reflected "the tragic and heroic experiences of our people," but as a sheltered Jewish child whose family (like many others) breathed nothing of the Holocaust to children, I did not know what to look for.

Orthodox Jews had a good many more texts to choose from when the company ArtScroll Mesorah launched its series of popular editions of Jewish sacred texts in 1975. Their Haggadot arrived with English-language commentaries and detailed instructions for every part of the seder, particularly concerning matters of Jewish law. Their Haggadot (now in over forty versions) appeals to a range of audiences, including children, families with many guests, and *ba'alei teshuvah* (Jews beginning to embrace Orthodox practice). Studying an ArtScroll Haggadah for the month before Passover prepares a seder leader with ample traditional insights to expound on. With ArtScroll, there are no ideological revolutions when it comes to the text itself; that is not subject to negotiation. The innovation is its high level of accessibility to Jewish tradition. It is of great appeal to those entering from the community's margins who benefit from transliterations and detailed instruction.

While some Haggadot of this era moved toward greater reconciliation with tradition. Others opened doors to more radical challenges to contents and purpose. But before we arrive at that place of the most contemporary creativity, we must linger in the twentieth century and face the most tragic era that the Haggadah has ever witnessed and chronicled, that of the Holocaust.

Haggadot of Darkness

Haggadot long reflected Jewish vulnerability. In kibbutz Haggadot we already glimpsed early responses to the Holocaust, including calls for rescue and plans for Jewish survival. Such Haggadot (and ones following their lead in Israel and elsewhere in the Jewish world) pressed the limits of what words and images could convey of raw grief, horror, near annihilation. Yet on the cusp of this darkest period of Jewish history, one Haggadah was created with no premonition of how fleeting the safety and comfort of Jews were. It assumed that next year's seder would be nowhere else but comfortably at home in Germany.

THE OFFENBACHER HAGGADAH

It was the 1920s, a period of Jewish renaissance in learning and art in Germany. Siegfried Guggenheim, a liberal Jew, lived in Offenbach, near Frankfurt am Main. This lawyer, art collector, and promoter of Jewish book arts set out to prepare a Haggadah inspired by the one created by Israel ben Moses in Offenbach in 1722, printed at the press of a gentile,

Bonaventura de la Nay. That earlier Haggadah represented a new elaboration on an older tradition, the very model of artistic innovation Guggenheim so fancied. Following convention, it reproduced the familiar copper engraved images of the 1695 Amsterdam Haggadah. But the creator of the 1722 edition produced no mere facsimile. He reverted to the earlier artistic technique: the woodcut. The result of this aesthetic choice was a new and modern work, fresh in its primitive spirit.

Guggenheim's own project represented the culmination of a loving, collaborative relationship with German calligrapher and typographic artist Rudolf Koch and the other artists of the cooperative workshop gathered around him (figure 5.1). Koch, who was not Jewish, described how congenial their making of the Haggadah was:

> It is the fundamental value of this work that a group of craftsmen created it together: calligraphers punch cutters, printers, wood engravers, and bookbinders. There was no direction of any person. They worked together as a unit, all in the same spirit, without detraction from their own feelings, and bound with strong ties of friendship and confidence to the author and editor.[1]

Guggenheim and Koch were friends for twenty-seven years, and their families regularly spent Christmas Eves together. These were times of laughter, singing, and wine drinking at the Koch home. One Christmas, Koch gave Guggenheim a dedicated copy of the exquisite volume of the Four Gospels he had designed, which was printed, as was the Haggadah, at the Klingspor Brothers Press.

Guggenheim envisioned his Haggadah appealing to the aesthetic tastes of book-loving German Jews and stirring the

FIGURE 5.1. Offenbacher Haggadah, 1927.

hearts of assimilated Jews to observe the Passover seder. It had Koch's new fonts in black and red and colorful illustrations by his student, the painter and graphic artist Fritz Kredel, in the style called Neue Sachlichkeit (new objectivity) that was eventually labeled degenerate art by the Nazis. The tastefully bound, three-hundred-copy edition of the Haggadah featured ample supplementary materials intended to make the book even more attractive to Guggenheim's target Jewish readership. Along with his translations into German, there were transliterations of the Hebrew blessings, musical notation for those who needed help with the melodies, and extensive explanations about the traditional text and its rituals. Adding *Gemütlichkeit* was a polite toast of gratitude to the "hausfrau," wishing this proverbial good woman of valor a long life.

When it came out, the Haggadah was well received by the Jewish press of Weimar, which celebrated it for demonstrating solidarity between German Jewry and German culture. This relationship, Guggenheim took as a given. What makes the edition particularly arresting as an artifact of the era of deep cultural assimilation is a note Guggenheim inserted, ironic and poignant in retrospect. It read:

> The Haggadah Manuscript preserved in the Germanisches Museum in Nuremberg, created in the year 5252 (or 1492 in our customary reckoning) by the *German* scribe Joel ben Rabbi Simon for Nathan ben Rabbi Salomo adds to the words *leshana haba b'yerushalayim* (next year in Jerusalem) the addendum, *or in Brünn*. The author, we assume, was probably expelled with the Jews from Brünn in 1454, and here in his old age, he gives moving expression to his longing for the home he was forced to leave in his youth.[2]

In other words, they yearned for both Jerusalem and their lost home in Brünn. Guggenheim, in his Haggadah, also expressed the traditional hope for next year in Jerusalem. But he concluded with an additional practice of his own family. Next year in Jerusalem was a pious sentiment. For now, they were celebrating their happiness in being rooted just where they were. With assurance, the Guggenheims proclaimed, "Next year in Worms-on-the-Rhein, our homeland (*heimat*)."

As it happens, Guggenheim's level of confidence in his homeland and the absence of fearful premonition were recently echoed in a 2011 interfaith Haggadah by popular American writers and journalists Cokie and Steve Roberts. In his introduction, Steve Roberts explained,

> The Seder's traditional ending is "Next year in Jerusalem," and if that phrase is meaningful to you, by all means use it. But we don't. For many American Jews, especially those in interfaith relationships, celebrating Passover in Israel is not a deeply held desire. We say, "Next year in Bethesda." For us, it's a more honest hope that reflects our real lives.[3]

The text of the Robertses' Haggadah eliminated reference to an earthly or heavenly Jerusalem. There is no hint of the historical fragility of Jewish well-being, forced dislocations, or Jerusalem signifying the brotherhood of all who yearn to be released from exile. Safety in one's country appears as the birthright of this American Jew and his partner: "We have celebrated in freedom and friendship. May we do so again next year, all of us together, with joy and peace."[4]

Returning to our story, in 1933, the year of the Nazi ascent to power, Guggenheim was forbidden to practice as a notary and was forced to dissolve his legal partnership. By 1938, he, like other German Jews, could no longer practice law. Following the infamous countrywide orchestrated pogrom of the night of November 9, 1938, now known as *Kristallnacht*,

Guggenheim was deported with other Jews and was interned briefly in Buchenwald. When released, he fled to New York. There, he eventually published a second edition of the original Haggadah in German and Hebrew with less arresting illustrations by artist Fritz Kredel, who had also found refuge in New York. This 1960 Haggadah, which included a prayer for the new State of Israel, had a significant and hardly surprising exclusion: reference to any place whatsoever in the diaspora as a first or second homeland that one either longs for or happily inhabits. Guggenheim's old family custom was pointedly forgotten. Celebrants were instructed to conclude the service with "Next year in Jerusalem," saying it emphatically, with full voice, and in intense alignment with the traditional Jewish longing for return, the very one Guggenheim now recalled being expressed in his father's house in order "to make our frames, our hearts, our minds more strongly still reverberate with that fundamental idea of our religion: The hope of the Messianic times, an age of peace."[5]

In a 1953 draft of a preface for an English version, Guggenheim explained: "It was the perspicacity of that great essayist, Stefan Zweig, that made him the first to point out in a letter (sent to the author shortly before Zweig took his own life) that an English edition should be greeted with general approval in the U.S.A."[6] But Guggenheim hesitated; could a translation do justice to the cataclysmic changes the Jewish world had endured in the years following the publication of his Haggadah? Despite misgivings, Guggenheim was persuaded that English would be the language used most by Jews, and he worked on the project for over fourteen years. To save popular German Passover tunes from oblivion, he gave them English words. Still he tried to retain the high tone of the German original. To the best of my knowledge, this Haggadah was never published. I hope it will be one day, as multiple drafts—literally cut-and-paste versions—remain among the boxes of Guggenheim's collected papers in the Leo Baeck archives in New York. In his later years Guggenheim continued to yearn for his lost life in Offenbach. When he died in 1961, he was cremated and buried there, testimony to the persistence of his longings for the spirit of his home and the once-idyllic artistic period that his first Haggadah represented.

The Szyk Haggadah

Unlike the Offenbacher Haggadah, the Haggadah of Arthur Szyk (pronounced "shick") was laden with premonitions of violence, frank in its representation of the dangers of the moment, and forthright as a warning to Jews to defend themselves. Szyk, born in Łódź, Poland, in 1894, was trained as a graphic artist and illustrator in Paris and Kraków and lived as an activist artist in France and England. He eventually found a home in the United States after World War II, where he was a well-known supporter of progressive political causes. Back in 1934, when he started work in Poland on his Haggadah, he was already known for his political cartoons and caricatures alerting the world to the threat of the Nazis and the plight of the Jews.

The images of Szyk's Haggadah recall the bright pages of detailed illuminated medieval manuscripts (figure 5.2).[7] They shimmer in jeweled colors as does the decorated calligraphy, based on a seventeenth-century Haggadah of his

FIGURE 5.2. The Szyk Haggadah, 1935.

birthplace. They are also ghoulish and disorienting, sharing qualities of the ornate, obsessively detailed illustrations Szyk later created for children's stories such as *Andersen's Fairy Tales*, where the beautiful and the grotesque sit side by side. (I still recall childhood nightmares stirred by the horrifying webs that spiders spun around the feet of "The Girl Who Trod on a Loaf.")

In this Haggadah, lauded by *The Times* of London as one of the most beautiful books ever produced, Szyk gave witness to the tragedy Jews faced. A proud but not religiously observant Jew, he resolved to serve his people with his artistic gifts. Painting swastikas on Egyptian characters, he linked Hitler to Pharaoh, the Egyptians to the Nazis. Even after fearful publishers compelled him to paint over the swastikas, his analogies remained evident. With pyramids in the background, Szyk connected the degraded Jews of Europe, portrayed in chains, to the Israelite slaves. Downtrodden in both eras, they reached out for elusive help. Szyk strongly advocated that Jews defend themselves in present times as they had in the biblical past. In the pages of his edition Szyk depicted classical Jewish heroes such as Moses, King David, and Judith who fought back against their oppressors with violence and vanquished them. He believed in modern-day Jewish resistance—and believed in revenge.

Szyk fully endorsed the Zionist enterprise. In his Haggadah, he portrayed young pioneers setting off for Israel—we know their destination from the image of oranges they are poised to harvest. Their departure is blessed by a withered religious elder who remains behind, emblematic of a past that can only be jettisoned.

The Haggadah of forty-eight watercolor and gouache paintings was completed in 1937, and Szyk supervised its production in London. At a cost of $500, it was considered at the time the most expensive book in the world. A luxury version published by Beaconsfield Press was dedicated to King George VI and given to him; the king kept it in his chambers and was proud to show it off. Its dedication page read, "At the feet of your most gracious majesty I humbly lay these works of my hands, shewing forth the afflictions of my people Israel." Depicted were the homeless Jews of Europe, old and young, yearning for a Zion they could reach if only His Majesty would come to their rescue and lift the British embargo on Jewish immigration to Palestine. Szyk, in effect, signed the plea, for he depicted himself at the bottom corner of the page, standing with an artist's palate in hand.

HAGGADOT FROM MEMORY

In many oral testimonies and written narratives of the Holocaust, Haggadot have played the role of touchstone. A recurring image is the seemingly miraculous Haggadah, smuggled into the bunks of a concentration camp just in time for Passover. In one testimony, a woman who was interned in a labor camp in Poland recalled holding on to the Haggadah given to her as a birthday present by her father. It was the only thing she had from before the war. She defiantly risked her life to preserve it, and she succeeded. Further, because of the Jewish education she had been given, unusual for a daughter, she was able to use it to conduct a seder for other girls.[8]

Recurring as well is the image of an absent Haggadah, written down or recited from memory for seders held under great risk, whether in ghettos, among partisans, in forests, in concentration or DP camps. One such story was told of the Hasidic Jews interned at Bergen-Belsen who had petitioned the camp commandant for flour to bake Passover matzahs, knowing this request could endanger their lives. Their leader, the Rabbi of Bluzhov, was summoned to appear before the commandant. To everyone's shock, permission was granted to bake matzah from rationed flour. As the rabbi recalled, they had baked three matzahs, but no "roasted shankbone, no egg, no haroset, no traditional greens, only a boiled potato given by a kind old German who worked at the showers." There was no Haggadah either, but he knew it by heart, and recited it from memory. A child asked why on this night there was matzah, but on all other nights, there was neither bread nor matzah. Typical of such narratives, the Passover story was parsed in accordance with their desperate lives and their longings, and the rabbi said,

> We have reached the depths of the abyss, the nadir of humiliation. Tonight we have only matzah, we have no moments of relief. . . . But do not despair, my young friends. . . . We who are witnessing the darkest night of history, the lowest moments of civilization, will also witness the great light of redemption.[9]

In another story of a Haggadah recited from memory, Israel I. Cohen wrote that on the night before Passover in Auschwitz, he and others went to sleep recalling past observances of the holiday before the war. He reflected pragmatically on his current situation, saying:

> Well, we can't fulfill the commandments of eating matzah and bitter herbs—but we really don't need any bitter herbs to remind us of the bitterness the Jews suffered in Egypt. Could theirs have been worse than ours? Impossible! Let us at least say the Haggadah, whatever we remember by heart.

In low voices, they chanted whatever they could remember. Others hearing them said, "What are you . . . doing, saying the Haggadah? Do you have matzos, do you have wine and all the necessary food to make a seder? Sheer stupidity!" In his account Cohen imagined God gladly accepting this secretive and improvised seder. This is a common trope in Jewish stories of piety: God's gracious acceptance of rituals performed in an unconventional manner by those of pure heart under duress.

> We are fulfilling the commandment of the Almighty to relate tonight the story of the Exodus from Egypt. If we don't have all the necessary accompaniments, it is not our fault, and we are not commanded to do the impossible. And who knows which seder is more welcome in Heaven, our seder in the dark and on empty stomachs . . . or the seder of our brothers in the United States and other countries that are not under the German's boots.[10]

A similar story came from Thomas S., a child in Bergen-Belsen. Asked if he had taken part in a seder, he replied, "Well, yes we did have a seder—a sawed-off seder . . . because we didn't have all the ingredients. We did the praying, we did the talking, we did the recounting, and we did the praying that we should be saved from this hell."[11]

One especially moving story of a hidden and then retrieved Haggadah comes from Werner Coppel, a German Jewish escapee from Auschwitz. Returning to Berlin in 1945 he uncovered, among other religious objects, a Haggadah buried in the Jewish cemetery in Weissensee. He never knew whose Haggadah it was or who buried it, but he used it to lead a seder for survivors of the Terezín (Theresienstadt) concentration camp at a Jewish old age home in Berlin in 1945. He and his wife took it with them to America, where they began new lives. As survivors who continue to give testimony, they still speak of it.[12]

Haggadot that were created from memory during and after the war years have a particular status; beyond being liturgical texts, they are also Holocaust artifacts. In their preciousness as Jewish objects from a world in which so much was destroyed, they take on some qualities of the sacred relic, particularly when they are exhibited in memorial museums or kept within families and passed on, as heritage items that represent more than what they are at face value. As such, they take on an aura that is more powerful and far reaching than any historical Haggadah. They are treated as material survivors—as objects haunted by memory. They resist complete interrogation, and the stories that they hold inside them may remain but partially known.

Before Passover of 1941, one such Haggadah was made and duplicated, apparently in Toulouse, for the thousands of German and foreign Jews incarcerated in the Vichy detention camp in Gurs, in the south of France. It was handwritten on stencils from memory, with only small mistakes, by Aryeh Ludwig Zuckerman, and it was edited by the camp's chaplain, Rabbi Leo Ansbacher. This Haggadah, which begins with a little drawing of a seder plate, consists of just five pages in Hebrew and another page of seder songs typed in transliteration. Limited editions included watercolor paintings of the Gurs camp made by a non-Jewish inmate, Karl Schwesig, later killed at Auschwitz. Some of these were sent outside the camp to give testimony to the harrowing conditions. Today, several copies of the Gurs Haggadah survive,[13] including one discovered in a box in the archives at Yad Vashem in Jerusalem, and another in a genizah in England. Zuckerman had escaped with the help of a friend, a French gravedigger who had hidden him in a coffin. He lived to raise a son who had become a rabbi. The son asked his father why he had shortened the particular section of the Haggadah from the Psalms, which begins "Pour out your wrath upon the nations." He had written only the word "Pour," eliminating the rest. Was it for lack of paper? No, the father explained, it was symbolic. While he felt that Nazis should be destroyed, he chose to refrain from a full expression of vengeance and hatred. Their fate, he trusted, would be decided by God alone.

Stories about Haggadot of memory also emerged from Russia, during the long period of Soviet persecution of Jewish life and culture. When Natan (then Anatoly) Sharansky marked Passover during his thirteen years of imprisonment in Siberia as a Jewish dissident, he recited psalms he knew from heart as well as the parts of the Haggadah he could recall—in particular the phrase "Today we are slaves, next year we will be free."

And stories of rescued Haggadot continue to emerge. The 2013 exhibit *Discovery and Recovery: Preserving Iraqi Jewish Heritage* at the National Archive in Washington, DC, displayed documents belonging to the Jewish community in Iraq that were found, by chance, by US Marines in the flooded basement of Saddam Hussein's intelligence headquarters in Baghdad during the futile search for nonexistent weapons of mass destruction. Among the thousands of artifacts were a 1902 Haggadah handwritten by an Iraqi youth and a colorful 1939 Haggadah from Vienna. These may have been collected by Saddam's secret police gathering information about Iraqi Jews, most of whom had already fled. The waterlogged documents were brought to the United States with the permission of the post-Saddam Iraqi government. Conservators froze, restored, and treated them for mold and heat. They were then digitized for free access.[14] Following traveling exhibitions, the tentative plan is to return them to Iraq if their safety can be ensured. The plan is controversial, as it has been argued that the artifacts, including the Haggadot, belong not to Iraq but to Jews of Iraq who were expelled from their country.

A Survivor's Haggadot

Directly after the war, Haggadot were written for the Palestine Jewish Brigade and Jewish soldiers in the many places where they served. "We are sitting together for a Passover Seder in Italy in the conquered city of Foggia, Jewish soldiers from Eretz Israel . . . and brothers who survived for whom it is the first Passover after years of suffering," reads one page of the 1944 Haggadah of Jewish Transportation Unit 179, Y.A.L. Italy/Provincia di Foggia, and "we must remember the millions who were murdered." Often told is a story concerning the Haggadah made by American soldiers in Dahn, Germany, who used Nazi flags as rags to clean the printing press.

Yosef Dov Sheinson, a Lithuanian Hebrew teacher who had been a slave laborer in the war, created a Hebrew and Yiddish Haggadah for the first seders of displaced Jews in Munich held at the Deutsches Theater restaurant in 1946. This was just one of many seders held by survivors. According to bibliographer Yaari, the Haggadot that were made available for survivors had been printed in Israel, England, the United States, Germany, and Holland. Sheinson's text was published by Zionist organizations (the initial arrangement entailed a payment of cigarettes and food rations); a later version was reprinted by the US Army occupying southern Germany for seders in DP camps. American army chaplain Rabbi Abraham J. Klausner, remembered for valiant work on behalf of stateless survivors, conducted the seders, understanding how important they would be for the survivors' morale. The text, with a red "A" on its cover, symbol of the Third Army, was discovered (and subsequently edited in a facsimile edition) by Saul Touster, a Brandeis professor who found it among the papers of his late father, once president of the Hebrew Immigrant Aid Society. Today, two copies of the original Haggadah can be found where I saw them, among the rare books of the Jewish Theological Seminary.

The Haggadah that Sheinson arranged, illustrated, and edited was by no means conventional. He called it a supplement, signifying its nontraditional nature. With script as jagged as barbed wire, it reflected both the Passover story and the losses of homeless survivors, forbidden from making their way to America or to Palestine. Written in Hebrew and Yiddish, and with "We were slaves to Hitler in Germany" as both theme and epigraph, its border images of gas "showers," crematoria, skulls, and smokestacks depicted the shared hardships and violence endured by both enslaved Israelites and the interned Jews. Additional woodcuts by Miklós Adler, a Hungarian survivor, depicting harrowing scenes, such as Nazis murdering Jews in cold blood on a forced march. One might ask, wouldn't children looking at the images of that Haggadah at the seder be further traumatized? In fact, Saul Touster learned in his research that when it came time at the Munich seder for the Four Questions, there was not a single child present to ask them. The response in the hall was a stunned silence, followed by weeping, and finally, the necessity for adults to ask the questions. The answers to the questions mocked tradition: "Why the bitter herbs?" This was Sheinson's self-castigating response:

> Because we were intoxicated by the incense of Galut
> (Diaspora)
> because we fled from one Galut (exile) to another,
> because we reassured ourselves saying: Ours will not
> be the fate that
> befell our people before us.
> Because we did little to help ourselves and reestablish
> our destroyed homes and country.[15]

If God had rescued the Jewish slaves and brought them to a safe haven—the thrust of the Haggadah's framing of the Exodus narrative—God did not come to save the Jews this time; Sheinson made that quite clear. Only the liberators came as saviors, and so late at that. Sheinson's parody of *Dayenu* came as an indictment. For all that had been permitted to go on, God was responsible:

> Had he given us Hitler but not ghettos, we would have been content. Had he given us ghettos but not gas chambers and crematories, we would have been content. Had he given us gas chambers and crematories but our wives and children had not been tortured, we would have been content.[16]

Sheinson's text affirmed his conviction that there was but one way Jews could protect themselves. They must settle in

Israel and rid themselves of the illusion that life anywhere else was feasible.

LITURGICAL ADDENDA

Berel Lang once wrote that since Jews were obliged to tell the story of slavery in Egypt as if they too had been there, at this juncture in history they are also obliged to tell the story of the Nazi genocide, for their extermination was intended as well. In the decades following the Holocaust, in Israel and in the diaspora, new liturgies were inserted into Haggadot to accommodate the reverberations of mourning and to create a place for rituals for remembrance, not just for survivors, but for all. Supplementary new liturgies appeared as gestures that might work toward repairing the breach in cosmic and social coherence.

Beginning in 1953, the American Jewish Congress mailed thousands of copies of a memorial liturgy in Hebrew and English for the murdered Holocaust victims to synagogues and Jewish organizations in an ambitious campaign to establish a shared American communal response to the Holocaust. They called it "The Seder Ritual of Remembrance for the Six Million Jews Who Perished at the Hands of the Nazis and for the Heroes of the Ghetto Uprisings." This ritual proposed invoking the victims by standing, as Jewish mourners do, during a recitation of the prayer for the dead. The turgid liturgy was reminiscent of the sections of midrash in the Haggadah, with reference to biblical proof-texts:

On this night of the seder we remember with reverence and love the six millions of our people of the European exile who perished at the hands of a tyrant more wicked than the Pharaoh who enslaved our fathers in Egypt. Come, said he to his minions, let us cut them off from being a people, that the name of Israel be remembered no more. And they slew the blameless and pure, men and women and little ones. . . . But we abstain from dwelling on the deeds of the evil ones lest we defame the image of God in which many was created.[17]

The liturgy concluded with the singing of *Ani Ma'amin* (I Believe), taken from Maimonides's Thirteen Principles of Faith. As the story goes, the music was composed by Rabbi Azriel-David Fastag as he was deported from Warsaw to his death in Treblinka. Those on the cattle car with him joined in, and it was sung in concentration camps by those being taken to the gas chambers. Today, it is sung at Holocaust memorial services:

> I believe with perfect faith in the coming of the
>   Messiah
> And though he may tarry, nonetheless, I shall wait
>   for him.

Despite the many copies of the ritual that were sent out, publishers of new postwar Haggadot did not take up this particular liturgy in the numbers that had been expected. In part, it was because its creators were adamant that it remain intact and unedited. But I think there was another reason. Resisting materials that might have felt too swiftly

canonized, creators of new Haggadot in the liberal denominations wanted to think through and craft their own
emerging responses to the Holocaust. The work of con-
structing post-Holocaust theologies they and their communities could embrace in good faith was part of the be-
reavement process, and this happened, in part, through
figuring out how to recognize the Holocaust and the establishment of the State of Israel in new Haggadot. What
should be said? Where should the text be placed? On what
images should attention be focused?

The 1982 Conservative Haggadah introduced its solution: "Both the Holocaust and the rebirth of the State of
Israel are mirrored here, for they shape our own Exodus
from our own Mitzrayim."[18] This Haggadah evoked the
mirroring with the abstract image of a broken matzah: on
one side are silhouettes of dark, huddled figures, and on the
other side are blue, white, and red figures marching under
the banner of the blue and white Israeli flag. Are the red
figures American Jews supporting Israel? Intentionally or
not, references to both the Holocaust and the State of Israel in postwar Haggadot, including this one, affirmed the
linkage between the memory of bondage under Nazis and
freedom in the State of Israel. There had been obvious tem-
poral reasons for experiencing the two historical events as
paired, and a logistical one as well—the State of Israel provided a haven for Jewish refugees. It was also natural to mit-
igate horror by giving it closure within the redemptive ending of the Passover story, to step back and see a broad
pattern of exile followed by return, instead of the specific
details. A possible result of the practice, and a particular
source of anxiety in Holocaust studies, was that the discrete

events, if paired in ritual, could lose their uniqueness. There is also the matter of a facile use of theology in the linking of these discrete events; it has been all too easy to implicate God in the most recent Jewish suffering and to see nationhood as deliverance. Further, marking the Holocaust on a holiday celebrating redemption had the unintended consequence of presenting the Holocaust as redeemable. Scholar Liora Gubkin, reflecting on Holocaust memory as portrayed in American Haggadot, saw that move as being akin to forgetting.[19]

The situation was different in America's Orthodox Jewish communities, where leaders have resisted inserting references to the Holocaust into Haggadot. One Orthodox rabbi explained that he was duty bound to refrain from incorporating the American Jewish Congress's "The Seder Ritual of Remembrance" text unless he were directed to do so by his generation's leading Orthodox rabbis. The Haggadah, he explained, should be concerned exclusively with telling about the exodus from Egypt; there was no place for sequels. Moreover, as Passover was for joy, a Haggadah should not engender sorrow. The Holocaust remembrance surely needed to find its place in the Orthodox community, but it would be found elsewhere, perhaps in a dirge recited on Tisha B'Av (Ninth of Av), the day of mourning marking the destruction of the First and Second Temples in Jerusalem.

Some Orthodox Jews, among them Polish-born Israeli scholar Rabbi Menachem Kasher (1895–1983), have proposed Haggadah innovations that make some reference to modern-day Israel. Kasher suggested drinking a fifth cup of wine, a practice with clear Talmudic origin, in thanksgiving for God's establishment of the State of Israel, seen as a sign of the beginning of redemption. While the Israeli rabbinate rejected Kasher's petition that the ritual be embraced as an official national practice, Rabbi Yitz Greenberg, a forward-thinking American Orthodox rabbi and noted Holocaust theologian, supported it. Given that Greenberg's own scholarship affirmed that Jewish tradition had never been static—and certainly not the Haggadah—he experimented with Haggadah inclusions of his own. In 1976, he urged that the *maggid* section (the narrative responding to the child's question) include prayers for the Jewish martyrs of Europe and Israel. A skillful ritualist and father of a large family, he noted that while the narrative should engage and be sufficiently vivid, it should not be "too long because people are hungry and the freedom meal is waiting."[20] In 1986, Greenberg published a Holocaust liturgy for the Haggadah along with his colleagues at the pluralist organization, CLAL, the National Jewish Center for Learning and Leadership, and disseminated it to his followers, both Modern Orthodox and liberal. This time, the ritual was linked, like Kasher's, to the fifth cup as "testimony that Israel's rebirth is revelation and redemption in our time. It is a statement of hope and trust that this is a lasting redemption which will not be destroyed again."[21] Affirming the coming of a messianic age that could be brought about only by Jews working in a voluntary partnership with God, it read, in part:

On this night, we remember a fifth child,
This is a child of the Shoah (Holocaust) who did not
    survive to ask.
Therefore, we ask for that child—Why?

... We answer that child's question with silence.
In silence, we remember that dark time.
In silence, we remember that Jews preserved their
    image
Of God in the struggle for life ...
(lift the cup of Elijah)
In silence, let us pass the cup of Elijah, the cup of the
    final redemption yet-to-be. ... Let us each fill
    Elijah's cup with some of our wine, expressing the
    hope that through our efforts, we will help bring
    closer that redemption.[22]

From the 1970s onward, seder leaders could find liturgies on the Holocaust mapped onto existing Passover paradigms in just about every liberal Haggadah. Certain types of readings that were liturgical in spirit were naturals for inclusion: Anne Frank's life-affirming passage from her diary about how "people are really good at heart"; excerpts from the writing of authors Primo Levi and Abraham Shlonsky; eyewitness accounts of the Warsaw ghetto uprising; passages from the work of Elie Wiesel; the names of the concentration camps and ghettos; excerpts from songs of the ghetto Partisans to affirm their heroism and resistance; and "Ani Ma'amin," to affirm continued belief.

Elie Wiesel's 1993 Haggadah was most deft in integrating Holocaust remembrance into the seder and most challenging as well. He was up front about the conundrum of combining suffering and celebration, noting the limits of language, and highlighting how redemption remains unfulfilled. Where better to place his reflection about the bitter and the sweet than within the ritual of Korech? This is the sandwich of bitter herbs, sweet charoset, and matzah, a practice of Temple days that was retained, even after the Temple had been destroyed:

> Present at the beginning of the story, God remains present to the end. The Seder, therefore, does not only tell the story of our suffering in exile, but also of our wait for redemption. And as we await redemption, the celebration of the word will yield to the celebration of the meal.[23]

Liora Gubkin recalls being horrified that in the published Haggadot of her childhood, readings about the Holocaust were presented as optional. Indeed, the readings cited the 1974 Conservative Haggadah (Anne Frank's words juxtaposed with Shlonsky's poem "The Vow," in which the poet vows never to forget his memories) were tagged with a little icon indicating they could be skipped. Gubkin asked, "How could the remembrance of the Holocaust be voluntary?"[24]

While the practice of mourning the victims of the Holocaust and making sense of it within the body of the Haggadah continues, I suspect it is in its last decades, particularly now that a designated Holocaust Remembrance Day is observed internationally. If there is to remain a conversation between the Haggadah and the Holocaust, it may be in the context of seder-inspired rituals held on Holocaust Remembrance Day, in which eggs dipped into ashes symbolize mourning, and turnips and potatoes are cast as bitter herbs recalling foods survivors would have known.

For the time being, the Holocaust remains present in Haggadot as a teachable moment, with only hints of the harshest memories evoked in texts that have, through their familiarity, lost some of their power to shock. Future-oriented vows are suggested: be vigilant over Jewish survival; take responsibility for all who are oppressed. References to the Holocaust have the character of digressions from the main business at hand, which for much of American Jewry means imparting on Passover eve a strong, effective, intellectually satisfying and positive dose of Jewish identity with the bare minimum of Jewish tragedy. I am thinking of *A Night to Remember: A Haggadah of Contemporary Voices* created in 2007 by father and son Noam and Mishael Zion,[25] in which the Holocaust memory is sparked by a carefully selected passage featuring the wartime memories of a kibbutz member who recalls the hunger of those years as she now breaks the seder matzah in half. The image selected to illustrate the theme is not horrifying; it is an Israeli postage stamp commemorating the Danish Christian underground for rescuing Danish Jewry and there are hopeful meditations by Anne Frank and Primo Levi. Here, even when the Holocaust appears, its presence is muted.

In a 2012 Haggadah of the Reform movement geared for contemporary families, attention to the Holocaust comes early in the seder, just after the Exodus story, and it serves to symbolize the pursuit of freedom. The Holocaust passage is inserted as a bare-bones history lesson, seemingly pitched to include those being introduced to the Holocaust for the first time: "Let us remember the Holocaust (in Hebrew: the Shoah), the dark days and nights of Adolf Hitler and Nazi Germany (1933–1945), where men, women, and children across Europe were murdered solely because they were Jewish."[26] A litany of names of concentration camps and ghettos are intoned by the leader, and then repeated by all, to honor the memory of not just Jewish victims, but also to recall "the many others who were killed because of their ethnic origins, sexual orientation, disabilities or political beliefs."[27] Here the ritual of remembering the Holocaust strengthens the resolve to take responsibility not just for Jews but for all persecuted peoples. Yet the illustrations by Mark Podwal in this Haggadah make no reference at all to the Holocaust; all the colorful images (with the exception of some unfortunate Egyptians) are festive; a menorah bursts forth with decorative flowers as cheerful as Marimekko fabric. By comparison, when Podwal illustrated Elie Wiesel's 1993 Haggadah, his black or maroon line drawings were haunting. In a macabre scene of historical destructions spreading forth from a Torah scroll in flames, the menorah Podwal drew was upside down, constructed of train tracks entering a concentration camp.

With Holocaust remembrance receding, other pressing concerns are becoming the foci of the Haggadah. Haggadot created and used by an ever-expanding group of seder-goers emphasize repairing Judaism and the world as well. People are still producing printed documents, and they are also projecting Haggadot onto screens or downloading them onto their digital devices. Each, on its own terms, claims it is a Haggadah. Where will all this innovation lead?

The Haggadah of the Moment

CHAPTER 6

Publishing Haggadot remains good business. So many come out each year that reviews of the newest ones are often playfully titled, "What makes this Haggadah different from all other Haggadot?" Perennial reviewer Jay Michaelson once organized the offerings into clever categories: marquee names (Haggadot edited by or otherwise associated with celebrity Jews); Passover for dummies (manuals explaining the basics of the seder for Jews and others with little Jewish education); coffee table Judaism (artistic editions for perusing or gifting); spiritual and earnest (thoughtful and accessible editions with the traditional text, transliteration, and commentary); and Jewish Pride (for those who "love the Jewish people first and foremost").[1] Spring 2015 was an especially prolific year. If you searched at bookstores or online, you could purchase: *Seder Talk: The Conversational Haggada*; *The Lieberman Open Orthodox Haggadah*; *The Unorthodox Haggadah: A Dogma-Free Passover for Jews and Other Chosen People*; *The Hasty Haggadah*; *The Monk's Haggadah: A Fifteenth-Century Illuminated Codex from the Monastery of Tegernsee*; *The Night That Unites Passover Haggadah: Teachings, Stories, and Questions from Rabbi Kook, Rabbi Soloveitchik, and Rabbi Carlebach*; and

The Baseball Haggadah: A Festival of Freedom and Springtime in 15 Innings. On my "be sure to check out" list for Passover of 2019 was Nina Paley's *The Seder Masochism: A Haggadah and Anti-Haggadah* (a companion book to her animated feature film, *Seder-Masochism*), which promised radical feminist commentary; I checked when it just came out and it was #1 among Haggadot on Amazon!

Each year there are also child-friendly versions sold in secular and religious bookstores. They have run the gambit from *Sammy Spider's First Haggadah* (2006) to one for the bookish child with coffee-table tastes, Eric A. Kimmel's award-winning *Wonders and Miracles: A Passover Companion; Illustrated with Art Spanning Three Thousand Years* (2004). In 2017, there was *The (Unofficial) Hogwarts Haggadah*, offering the perspectives of Harry Potter himself. And in time for Passover of 2019, Maxwell House coffee produced *The Marvelous Mrs. Maisel Limited Edition Passover Haggadah*, a pink-colored "New 1958 version," complete with drawings of the cast of the Amazon Prime TV show, *The Marvelous Mrs. Maisel*, and an inserted recipe card for Midge Maisel's Brisket.[2]

Add to these the "speeded up" variety, pitched to adults whose seder attention span is about the duration of a TV comedy. There is *30-Minute-Seder Haggadah* (standard, downloadable, and Braille), billed as having rabbinical approval (the one approving rabbi is pictured). There's the *Ten Minute Seder* too. And then there is Michael Rubiner's "Two-Minute Haggadah: A Passover Service for the Impatient," which appeared in *Slate* on April 11, 2006. It was no doubt meant as a joke; did someone use it somewhere? Probably. In part, it reads:

The story of Passover: It's a long time ago. We're slaves in Egypt. Pharaoh is a nightmare. We cry out for help. God brings plagues upon the Egyptians. We escape, bake some matzoh. . . . We wander 40 years in the desert, eat manna, get the Torah, wind up in Israel, get a new temple, enjoy several years without being persecuted again. (Let brisket cool now.)[3]

Despite abundant published novelties, the lion's share of Haggadot sold in America appeal to conventional tastes. Still popular is the frequently updated 1949 Haggadah of Rabbi Nathan Goldberg, often bought in multiples of ten. (My "Hebrew School Haggadah"; with its numbered lines, my family often uses it at seders in addition to the new ones we pass out.) People are still using Schocken's 1979 *The Passover Haggadah*, edited by Nahum N. Glatzer; it reaches across denominations and its commentary doesn't intimidate seder novices. Best sellers are the content-rich Haggadot published and coauthored by Noam Zion. There's *The Family Participation Haggadah: A Different Night*, written with David Dishon, and *A Night to Remember: The Haggadah on Contemporary Voices*, which he wrote with his son Mishael. Popular among Sephardic families is *A Sephardic Passover Haggadah*, edited by Rabbi Marc C. Angel, formerly the rabbi of New York's Spanish and Portuguese Synagogue in New York, or *The Sephardic Heritage Haggadah*, edited by Rabbis Eli Mansour and David Sutton.

In Crown Heights, Brooklyn, home of the Lubavitch sect of Hasidic Jews, religious bookstores are filled annually with Haggadot for their followers of every inclination and background, from the householder to the learned scholar.

Elegance is acceptable: one Hasidic publisher offered a leather-bound edition in distinctive party-favor shades such as hot pink, pearl pink, turquoise, and light grape—to add "sparkle" to one's table and to serve as a conversation starter. A Lubavitch organization, Friends of Refugees of Eastern Europe (FREE), has been producing and distributing Hebrew-Russian Haggadot for over thirty-five years, going back to Soviet times when their Haggadah was the first sacred Jewish text published in modern Russian. Their Haggadah was created for Jews of the former Soviet Union, denied the freedom to study or practice Judaism. When I visited FREE, I was given a copy of their Russian Haggadah to add to my personal collection. I brought it with me to a meeting with the staff of the International Rescue Committee in Charlottesville, Virginia, to prepare them for an upcoming seder that that my University of Virginia students studying the Haggadah were planning to host on the theme of refugees becoming new Americans. As I passed various Haggadot around the room, one staff member, a woman who had been a refugee herself, stared at my Russian edition with astonishment. She kept holding on to it. After nearly everyone else had left the room, her eyes were still glued to its pages. "Keep it if you like," I said. I was not prepared for what she told me, or how bewildered she appeared. "It is all so familiar. My grandmother spoke Yiddish. She never explained why."

Israelis don't really need to invest in store-bought Haggadah texts because so many are distributed for free by newspapers, banks, and even the army. Still, bookstore displays of Haggadot spill out onto the sidewalks before the holiday. Some Israeli editions speak to the eye-rolling levity many secular Israelis bring to the Passover seder, even when their preferred text is the traditional one they find boring and impenetrable. One, a perennial favorite of children and parents since 1985, is *The Animated Haggadah*, based on a Claymation film made by Rony Oren; another that I love is a whimsical 2008 *Golan Heights Winery Haggadah*, once given away at the Supersol market with the purchase of two bottles of Yarden wine. The wise son in this Haggadah is a computer geek typing away at his laptop; an Israelite slave carries a refrigerator on his back as he crosses the sea; ancient rabbis of B'nei Brak scratch out Einstein's formula on a blackboard; Grandma in heaven tosses down gefilte fish into her family's open mouths; and a woman, having exhausted herself finding the answers to the song *Echad Mi Yode'a* (*Who Knows One?*) on her computer flops down onto a beanbag with a well-deserved glass of Yarden wine.

The market in artistic Haggadot remains lively in Israel, where every spring, potential Haggadah buyers can mill about at fairs at which famous Haggadah artists such as Avner Moriah, Maty Grünberg, Eliyahu Sidi, Matt Berkowitz, Ya'akov Boussidan, Asher Kalderon, and David Moss have shared their work and revealed how they created their fine arts editions.

No artistic Haggadah has yet gained as much attention worldwide as David Moss's celebrated work, commissioned by Richard and Beatrice Levy in 1980 and admired for its use of the Jewish art traditions of intricate paper cutting and microcalligraphy. It was then reproduced in three versions, called The Facsimile Edition, The Trade Editon, and The Deluxe Edition. Particularly admired is the illustration that accompanies the text: "In every generation one must see himself as having come from Egypt."

Moss has created a checkerboard with every other square filled with profiles of Jews worldwide through time. The in-between squares are mirrors in which readers can see themselves reflected as well.

In the past years, Daniel and Joanna S. Rose of New York, in search of the perfect edition for their own family, commissioned an illuminated Haggadah, selecting American and Israeli artisans renowned for their craftsmanship.[4] Barbara Wolff's artwork is inspired by the great medieval Haggadot and features a text written calligraphically on parchment, gilded first words and images, and a handmade binding. But there are modern touches, too, such as the mixture of English and Hebrew. Like other recent Haggadot of note, this one has its own video trailer documenting the research, the techniques that went into it, and expressing the patrons' hopes that the edition will be a source of Jewish continuity.[5] Members of the Rose family have already started using a facsimile version of this edition at their seder. In keeping with the recent launches of other artistically significant Haggadot, the original had its debut in 2015 in a public exhibition at the Morgan Library in New York. The plan was to house it there, never to be compromised by the rough seder table handling.[6]

At Passover time every spring since the 1970s, the Jewish and secular media have been heralding seders that address social issues. In 1998 Jan Hoffman called the cause-driven seder a "seder nouveau." There were "women's seders. Seders as Last Suppers. Cyberseders. Environmental seders. Gay seders. Secular seders. . . . Even (warning: you may want to avert your eyes) Fabulous seders, as in 'come dressed as your favorite plague.'" Each seder had its own new Haggadah created to suit the theme and the audience. The reception to the explosion of creativity was mixed:

> Some commentators say the activity reflects a millennium-end quest for spiritual values still grounded in a home-centered service and meal. Others say it is a neurotic by-product of a flourishing American Jewry that does not have a unifying external crisis like civil rights or the plight of Soviet Jews as a contemporary analog for the Exodus story of slavery and freedom.[7]

Even critics who disapproved of this free-form innovation in the service of worthy causes took pride in the phenomena. In the conservative Jewish journal *Commentary*, for example, Michael Medved acknowledged:

> There's something actually miraculous about Jews of every description and orientation coming back in some form or another to the same words and rituals. In the twenty-first century, we still use symbols, gestures, foods, and even wording our great-grandfathers would have recognized to push pet causes, from animal liberation to Buddhism to lesbian consciousness.[8]

The *New York Times* reported on a now-familiar rhetorical question: "Why is there an orange on the seder plate?" This question, now included in many Haggadot, started being posed at American Jewish seders in the late 1980s, prompting the telling of an apocryphal anecdote. As the story went, there was once a male rabbi who told a Jewish feminist scholar, Professor Susannah Heschel, that a woman belonged on the synagogue's *bimah* (podium) no more than an orange belonged on a seder plate. For American Jews who advocated gender equality in religious ritual, placing an orange on the plate was the rejoinder to the backward-thinking rabbi. Women *do* indeed belong, the orange broadcasts, not just as a synagogue leader, but in all spheres of Jewish life!

As the orange became entrenched in seder practice, new Haggadot wove together the apocryphal and factual versions of the orange's origins. They told the true story of how bread was once added to the seder plate at Oberlin College to symbolize lesbians feeling disenfranchised in their Jewish communities. That was followed by Heschel actually proposing a less transgressive symbol: a tangerine, whose seeds could be spit out to symbolize ejecting homophobia from Judaism. Oranges began appearing on seder plates, and of late, their presence is expansively parsed to represent not just empowered Jewish women but also a Judaism that welcomes diversity.

Creators of new Haggadot for these politically, socially, environmentally, and religiously engaged seders built on the historical precedent of kibbutz Haggadot and third seders. But they also were reflecting the democratic, do-it-yourself spirit of the Jewish counterculture of the late 1960s and 1970s.

One Haggadah emblematic of the beginning of this era was the *Freedom Seder*,[9] composed by Arthur Waskow back when he was a fiery young political activist. His influential countercultural Haggadah challenged presumptions about who had the right to create a Haggadah, what ends it could serve, and for whom it could have meaning. His *Freedom Seder* was first used on the third night of Passover of 1969 by eight hundred people: black and white, Jewish and Christian, who gathered in an African American, Washington, DC, church for a civil rights seder to honor the memory of Rev. Martin Luther King Jr., assassinated the year before. When word spread that this Haggadah included the words of Henry Thoreau, Eldridge Cleaver, Allen Ginsberg, and Gandhi, it elicited vitriol among the American Jewish establishment. They leaped to the conclusion that young Jewish student radicals were threatening Jewish tradition as a whole. The *Freedom Seder* Haggadah certainly took liberties, referring to Thoreau and Gandhi as rabbis (using the term in its broadest sense to mean, simply, "teacher"), calling Cleaver a *shofet* (judge) and Ginsberg a *tzaddik* (exemplar of righteous behavior). One could argue that Waskow's Haggadah was less a radical departure than a reframing of the Haggadah's inherently radical message of liberation. This was a powerful message for young Jews inclined to dismiss the Judaism of their parents as "irrelevant" or to take their spiritual longings elsewhere. The *Freedom Seder*, by its example, encouraged young people, including those "turned off" by the suburban Judaism of their parents, to engage with the ancient text and to make it their own.

Waskow eventually trained as a rabbi and became a leading figure in the Jewish Renewal movement. He prepared many more Haggadot, including a controversial 2013 edition aimed at provoking political action in response to global climate change. This Haggadah, launched by Waskow's Shalom Center organization during a pre-Passover/Holy Week "Interfaith Moral Action on Climate" in Washington, DC, reframed the ten plagues as ecological disasters such as fracking, drought, and superstorms. The Haggadah instructed participants to recite each modern-day plague and to respond with the word "sorrow," to be spoken after each plague. Healing solutions were then proposed to address the plagues, and as each was stated, the Haggadah recommended the affirmative response, "*L'chayyim, To life.*"

Creating organic farms in countrysides and cities. *(L'chayyim, To life!)*
Wind-based energy: Purchasing home & company electric power from wind-based suppliers. *(L'chayyim, To life!)*
Hybrid or electric cars. Families buy them; convince cities, government agencies, & businesses to switch their auto fleets. *(L'chayyim, To life!)*

Waskow's Washington seder concluded with civil disobedience at the White House gates. Waskow and the other celebrant-protestors who refused to move were arrested.[10]

Among liberal Orthodox Jews, promoting attention to social justice was achieved in a 2001 Haggadah supplement from the organization Uri L'Tzedek. It transformed the ritual of saying a blessing over the bitter herb (*maror*) and eating it into a highly detailed eight-step meditation. It begins, "Place the maror in your hand. While feeling the maror, reflect on the comfort level you are currently experiencing," and concludes with making "a realistic, tangible commitment to addressing the source of bitterness that you pictured in the world" and sharing "your commitment with the person next to you."[11]

Strategies for transforming one's seder evening commitment to social justice into concrete action were also imbedded in the Hunger Seder Haggadah, used for National Hunger Seders that are held to influence American policy makers and elected officials to address food insecurity.[12] To be sure

that the seder planners around the country engaged in opti-
mal preparation and follow-up, the Haggadah went beyond
the traditional fifteen seder steps. It provided a checklist of
instructions for local organizers, including a time line for
planning. There were ideas for who to invite (including
elected officials, people of different faiths, and representa-
tives of the food bank), where to hold it, how to promote
the event (having a "hook" helps, such as promising interfaith relationships or highlighting an important local issue),
how to contact the press (including prominent local blog-
gers), how to use social networking tools during the seder
(tweeting and sending Facebook posts), and how to follow
up with letters sent to members of Congress.

The Jewish American feminist movement of the 1970s,
protesting against misogyny and patriarchy in the Jewish tradition, gave rise not just to the orange on the seder plate but
also to many women-centered Haggadot. The seder, with its
capacity for ritualized expressions of critique and repair, presented itself as an ideal setting for airing and repairing gender
injustices. It was also, of course, a ritualized event associated
with generations of mothers and grandmothers slaving in the
kitchen for the days before Passover and, ironically, even during the seder itself, without ever finding a moment to sit down
at the table to recite verses about so-called liberation. Jewish
feminists designed Haggadot that aroused righteous indignation, demanded inclusion and respect, and challenged the
maleness of God. They brought women to the table by inserting women's wisdom into the Passover's "master" narrative
and by presenting worthy Jewish women as role models.

An early feminist Haggadah is the Rice Paper Haggadah,[13] less well known because there was (and still is) but a

single copy written on rice paper. It was originally created in 1971 by Jewish women in Portland, Oregon, and it was later transported to the Park Slope section of Brooklyn by one of the group, Bria Chakovsky. Its performance (which included the singing of folk music of the civil rights cause) in the brownstone of four women living together was chronicled in the women's liberation journal *Off Our Backs*. The Haggadah traveled with its "keeper" to Seattle, where it was revised for use in the large community seders for the progressive Jewish organization Kadima. I have a page of this historical artifact in my hands now, and with the owner's permission, I will submit it for safekeeping to the National Museum of American Jewish History. This page represents an early appearance of feminist midrash, that is, the telling of biblical stories about women from the perspective of contemporary women. Here, the story of slavery is narrated by a collective of women who speak in one voice:

> Now it happened that a group of women began meeting secretly to explore their lives and the sources of their isolation and oppression. They talked . . . and wept and wept and wept and smiled and laughed and hugged and loved and learned
>> about themselves
>> about each other
>> about their bodies . . .
>> about process
>> about pain
>> about anger.[14]

The best-known Haggadot that have addressed feminist issues were created by Jewish feminist activists learned in the tradition. *Lilith* magazine's Egalitarian Haggadah (1982), for example, was put together by Aviva Cantor, a writer, editor, and *Lilith* cofounder. Its innovations were considered radical at the time. God the King became a gender-neutral Ruler of the Universe, Jacob's wives were referred to by their names, and Four Daughters replaced the Four Sons. Another well-known feminist Haggadah first appeared in *Ms.* magazine in 1977, a collaboration of American writer E. M. Broner and Israeli writer Naomi Nimrod. After holding a feminist seder in Israel, they continued to deepen their study of Jewish sources to discover more about the women of the Exodus. They did this under the eye of Nimrod's mother, who initially had reservations about their enterprise, asking, "What are you doing? . . . The Haggadah is already written."[15] Their core text was introduced in 1976 at an annual feminist seder in New York City over which Broner, Phyllis Chesler, and Letty Cottin Pogrebin, among others, presided. Women's movement notables such as Bella Abzug, Gloria Steinem, and Grace Paley, dubbed "The Seder Mothers," were often in attendance at this annual event. Perhaps the most widely circulated and frequently consulted feminist Haggadah is a text once used (and brought home, for inspiration during one's family seder) by hundreds of women who gathered each year in New York City for the organization Ma'yan's annual women's seders enlivened by composer Debbie Friedman's music held between 1994 and 2005. There were successive versions[16] of the text created in large part by Tamara Cohen and Debbie Friedman, who presided together over the event.

Revolutionary consciousness-raising feminist Haggadot are now essentially a thing of the past. Gone is the outrage, the sense of crisis, and the urgency. When women's seders are now offered, if they are offered at all, they are scheduled as Sisterhood events at synagogues and colleges. The once-radical agenda is replaced by an upbeat celebration of Jewish women in history for mothers and daughters to share. Haggadot are patched together by committee, with sources only occasionally noted. De rigueur is an image of an orange on the seder plate, a cup of water for Miriam, and many tambourines, suggesting the miniature ones that will be passed around for dancing to Debbie Friedman's composition in homage to Miriam and the Israelite women. Table conversations are prompted: some version of "describe your liberation from a place of narrowness" (a literal translation of *mitzraim*, the word for Egypt). Women might be invited to explain small objects of their own journeys that they were instructed to bring from home, and touching stories will be spontaneously shared—but they rarely evoke the rebellious cries of the early feminist Haggadot, such as this one from the Broner/Nimrod Haggadah:

> Mother, asks the wicked daughter,
> If I learn my history, will I not be angry?
> Will I not be as bitter as Miriam
> Who was deprived of her prophecy?[17]

I asked Rabbi Rachel Barenblat what had propelled her to create new feminist Haggadot over the years, first as a college student and later, continuing to do so, as a rabbi. She explained that her relationship to Jewish tradition and its texts had shifted and she wanted a Haggadah that spoke to her. The process of periodic Haggadah-making accommodated her personal spiritual development, her changing social roles, and society's acceptance of once-radical ideas. When she was working on her first feminist Haggadah in college in the 1990s, she confronted gender issues by turning the masculine God-language into more inclusive language. But that still left issues of power unresolved, so in later Haggadot she eschewed hierarchical images for God entirely, replacing King and even Queen with terms such as Source and Wellspring. At present she has shared that she is comfortable with many ways of addressing God and finds that she has become more sensitive to balancing her desire to shake up established notions of the divine with the need to respect other people's preferred God-language. In her earliest days as a feminist, she was more interested in women's narratives and experience. Like many of her peers, she now embraces an integration of women's and men's stories, and her recent text, *The Velveteen Rabbi's Haggadah for Pesach*, is for everyone. She describes a comfortable meshing of the ancient and the modern: "I want a Haggadah which includes both the classical Hebrew and Aramaic texts I've learned to love, and the contemporary feminist poems and interpretations which have been such an important part of my Jewish awakening."[18]

The Formula

In addition to brand new published Haggadot, facsimiles of the modest and deluxe variety, reprints, and photo offsets, the uncountable number of extant new Haggadot now includes thousands of unique, community-tailored, photocopied homemade versions, and of late, even projected PowerPoint displays or personalized digitized versions, downloaded on tablets, electronic readers, and as apps for mobile phones.

They adhere to a loose formula. There is a pluralist table gathering, including people encountering a Haggadah and attending a seder for the first time. There is an oppressive and recent problem, and it is compared to the state of being enslaved. Moral indignation is aroused and education is offered. The solution to the problem emerges from an updated telling of the Exodus story. The steps of the traditional seder are followed more or less, with repurposed symbols evoked to bring the points home. If the liturgy works, participants leave emboldened, poised to act on their commitments and, often, to support the good works of the organization that provided the Haggadah.

New Haggadot often introduce unusual objects for the seder plate and table for particular symbolic reasons. In addition to the aforementioned oranges and tangerines, artichokes—with their prickly outer leaves and soft inner hearts—have been introduced as a symbol of welcome for interfaith families.[19] Chocolate and coffee beans show concern for children exploited in developing countries by these extractive industries.[20] In the same spirit, the tomato points to the plight of migrant workers,[21] and rotten pieces of lettuce and a single potato chip serve as graphic reminders of how difficult it is to come by healthy foods in low-income neighborhoods.[22] Roberta Kalechofsky's *Haggadah for the Liberated Lamb*, which calls itself both a Haggadah and a manifesto for vegetarians who seek to end cruelty to animals, suggests that if a roasted egg must be displayed on the seder table, it should at least come from a free range chicken. This Haggadah recommends replacing the shank bone and the ancient sacrifice of a lamb it represented with olives, grapes, and barley or other unfermented grain, parsed from biblical verses to represent the bounty of a free and charitable people.[23]

Most feminist Haggadot, in the same spirit, have introduced a Miriam's Cup, and the practice has caught on in family seders. This new ritual is linked to the legend that the biblical prophetess's presence among the wandering Israelites ensured that a miraculous well would appear for them. The cup—a complement to Elijah's cup of wine—is usually filled with water from everyone's cup. In addition to celebrating the prophetess Miriam as a song and dance leader known for her optimism and healing presence, it encourages celebrants to praise both important and everyday Jewish women for their inspiration and leadership.

Another drinking ritual innovation is found in the so-called sober seder. Participants celebrate a nonalcoholic Passover with grape juice, and the text of their Haggadah merges the liberation from slavery narrative with the recovering alcoholic's struggle against addiction.

In a similar vein, the 2008 *GLBT Haggadah*[24] calls for two seder plates, one traditional and a second one laden with a coconut, an orange, sticks and stones, flowers, pickled vegetables, and fruit salad. A previous edition of the *GLBT Haggadah* had eliminated the traditional plate altogether and replaced it with the one filled with novelties. This was not well received. It violated some people's holiday expectations, and the absence of comforting familiarity stood in the way of the overriding goal of addressing the pressing matter of gender and sexual equality. Back came the traditional seder plate in the revised second edition.

The coconut represents "those who are still locked inside their shell hiding from the world their inner beauty as an out and proud GLBT Jew" and evokes the liberating experience of having come out of the closet. The orange affirms the presence of all Jews who have felt marginalized and is meant to be eaten with an imagined piece of coconut. The orange-flavored charoset indicates how "queer Jews and others on the outskirts of the tradition" add their sweetness to the "mortar that binds our people." Slices of cucumber soaked in cider vinegar and lemon juice represent bigotry and homophobia. Fruit salad is about diversity enhancing the collective, flowers are about the beautiful path of life, and sticks and stones signify pain and anguish along the way (figure 6.1). (University of Virginia students studying the Haggadah with me put this one to the test. I anticipated they'd say the new plate, while now better positioned in the text, was overly busy, and the connection between the symbols, Passover and their new meanings, rendered in workaday prose, might seem tenuous. I was wrong; the students said that celebrating Passover with this new Haggadah and its seder plate was life-changing.)

In Israel, new supplements used recently to update traditional Haggadot have included the designation of empty chairs for those held captive or endangered, a theme in keeping with a Jewish tradition from Yemen. An empty chair was designated to represent a captive soldier, Gilad Shalit, during a seder held outside the Israeli prime minister's residence at the time of Shalit's imprisonment by Hamas as a protest against the government's failure to address his captivity. In recent years, Israeli refugee Haggadot have appeared that bring awareness to the plight of African

FIGURE 6.1. Seder plate with coconut, an orange, sticks and stones, flowers, pickled vegetables, and fruit salad.

refugees who seek sanctuary in Israel but remain at risk of harassment and deportation.

In the first spring of Donald Trump's administration, inserts for Haggadot strengthened the resolve of those who opposed his efforts to bar refugees. A HIAS 2016 Supplement, suggested the traditional ten plagues be followed by a ten plagues of today:

> Remembering the ten plagues that God brought upon the Egyptians when Pharaoh refused to free the Israelites, we have the opportunity tonight to recognize that the world is not yet free of adversity and struggle. This is especially true for refugees. After you pour out a drop of wine for each of the ten plagues that Egypt suffered, we invite you to then pour out drops of wine for ten modern

plagues afflicting refugee communities worldwide and in the United States. After you have finished reciting the plagues, choose a few of the expanded descriptions to read aloud.

1. Violence
2. Dangerous journeys
3. Poverty
4. Food insecurity
5. Lack of access to education
6. Xenophobia
7. Anti-refugee legislation
8. Language barriers
9. Workforce discrimination
10. Loss of family[25]

Using humor strategically as a means of political protest, there was Jacob Alperin-Sheriff's satirical *The Republican Haggadah*—5777 edition, which includes a version of the song *Adir Hu* that went like this:

> *May he soon Build The Wall,*
> *Speedily, speedily and in our days, soon.*
> *Donald, build, Donald build,*
> Build the wall with Mexico!

Or finally, his version of the song *Echad Mi Yode'a* (Who Knows One?)

> *Who knows seven? I know seven! Seven are the countries of the Muslim ban, and six are the Goldman Sachs alumni in the Trump administration, and three are the millions of illegal Democrat voters, and two are the unfaithful electors,*

*and one is Donald Trump, one is Donald Trump, one is
Donald Trump, only he can fix it.*[26]

The most provocative and liturgically successful Haggadah I have used in recent years was created by maverick Rabbi
Amichai Lau-Lavie, known for his inventiveness, theatrical-
ity, and challenges to oppressive communal norms. Its title,
The Sayer, part English and part Hebrew, puns on the idea
that there is so much to *say* at a seder.[27] His friends in New
York City had invited him to design a second night's seder
that would not be a tedious repetition of the traditional one
most had observed on the night before. He told me that
practically on the spot, he created a version preserving storytelling, conversation, and an optimistic spirit. At its heart are
four questions. They assume some Judaic literacy—at least
knowing the Exodus story and the Haggadah's key passages.
The instructions are simple:

> The host leads the guests in four rounds of questions
> and answers. Each round features one question, one re-
> fill of wine, and one topic. Food is served between
> rounds, leading up to the main Passover feast. Guests
> and hosts can insert traditional Seder readings, songs,
> and personal stories.

Its new questions and topics combine the outward-looking
perspective of activist Haggadot with the self-actualization
characteristic of feminist seders:

> 1. MA NISHTANA: WHAT'S NEW: What signifi-
> cant change has occurred in your life since this time
> last year? Name one meaningful piece of news.

2. AVADIM HAYENU: OUR SLAVERY: Identify the problem. What enslaves you today? What's holding you back from being freer, happy, and creative?

3. DAYENU: ENOUGH: Identify possible solutions. What can you do to help end your enslavement and reduce that which holds you back from more freedom and creativity? What will help you fight the Pharaohs within?

4. L'SHANA HA'BAA: FUTURE VISION—NEXT YEAR: We can't end the Seder until we all commit to making the world a better place, with less oppression and more freedom. What is your vision of a freer world? What do you commit to in the coming year to help reduce slavery and oppression in the world?[28]

How will any of these new Haggadot be remembered by future generations? Their liturgies are not always eloquent, and while the better supported ones are professionally designed, many rely on the cut-and-paste process of desktop publishing. The issues that matter in one season are replaced by newer issues the media has taken up. What will endure, I believe, is the conviction that undergirds them all: the wisdom of Jewish traditional texts and practice can illuminate the complexity of current issues and press people to become agents of change.

In my class on the Passover Haggadah the students come from all kinds of backgrounds. It's a community engagement course, which means that in addition to students' historical studies of the Haggadah, they are required to volunteer with a community agency. The last month of the semester, the students create their own Haggadah, which addresses the agenda of their agency and the needs of its clients. They have created Haggadot addressing hunger, ecology, feminism, coming out, disordered eating, interfaith relations, the plight of migrant workers in Virginia, the challenges of establishing roots as a refugee. There was once a Paleo Haggadah, and I have held on to the pop-up Haggadah that gently introduced children to death. I don't give quizzes, but if I did, by the time the course concludes, my students can ace this one:

(a) Who may write a Haggadah?
(b) Who can make changes to the traditional Haggadah?
(c) What situations justify making a Haggadah?

Answers:

(a) Anyone with a computer
(b) Anyone
(c) All

From Page to Stage and Screen

From the beginning of the modern era, the lyrics of beloved Passover holiday songs were included in print Haggadot; *Echad Mi Yode'a* (Who Knows One?) and *Chad Gadya* (An Only Goat) were both in the 1695 Amsterdam Haggadah. Now, just about every new Haggadah, whether professionally published or homemade, still contains those lyrics, and sometimes musical notes too. The Haggadah has preserved these songs, and now, in the contemporary era, they are leaping from page to stage and screen. Here are selections from the lyrics:

From *Echad Mi Yode'a*:

> Who knows thirteen?
> I know thirteen.
> Thirteen are the attributes of God;
> Twelve are the tribes of Israel;
> Eleven are the stars of Joseph's dream;
> Ten are the Commandments;
> Nine are the months of pregnancy;
> Eight are the days of circumcision;
> Seven are the days of the week;
> Six are the books of the Mishnah;
> Five are the books of the Torah;
> Four are the Matriarchs;
> Three are the Patriarchs;
> Two are the tablets of the covenant;
> One is our God, in heaven and on earth.

From *Chad Gadya*:

> Then came the Holy one, blessed be He
> And smote the angel of death,
> Who slew the slaughterer,
> Who killed the ox,
> That drank the water,
> That extinguished the fire,
> That burned the stick,
> That beat the dog,
> That ate the goat
> Which my father bought for two zuzim.
> One goat, one goat.

A little background on these folk songs, first. The genealogy is fuzzy. They are most likely adaptations of popular ballads, and while they originated in the Ashkenazi tradition, they were adapted by Sephardim as well. *Echad Mi Yode'a* is a number game. It depicts a knowable and orderly universe beginning with the unity of God and ending with God's multiple yet numerable attributes. In contrast, *Chad Gadya* (believed to have been written originally in Judeo-German and then translated into a flawed Aramaic) represents a chaotic world in which the only predictable forces are power and violence. With each verse, a bully is vanquished, one by one, until God's breaking of the cycle at the end with an ultimate killing.[29] *Chad Gadya* is often described as an allegory. If the young goat represents the Jews who are the victims, and the two coins (*zuzim*) are the two tablets of the Ten Commandments, then each subsequent predator is yet another historical enemy (Assyrians, Babylonians, Persians, and so forth) who tried but failed to destroy the Jews. Ultimately, God alone can restore order by vanquishing death or undoing it through resurrection in the end of days.

Here is how the lives of these songs have extended beyond both Haggadah and seder. *Echad Mi Yode'a* was choreographed by Ohad Naharin in 1990 for Israel's renowned contemporary dance group, the Batsheva Ensemble, and is now performed around the world by dance professionals and amateurs alike. In the original production, the dancers sit in a circle of chairs costumed in kibbutz work clothes. Other productions have had them dressed in the black suits, white shirts, and black hats typical of ultra-Orthodox Jews. (In a Japanese performance, they were thought to represent stockbrokers.) The music, which fuses a traditional *Echad Mi*

Yode'a with a pulsating rock soundtrack, gets faster and more frenzied, as does the dance. The dancers alternate tense stillness with a growing collection of angular and explosive synchronized movements. The end of each verse—which includes the mention of God's name—is accompanied by the collapse of a dancer to the floor. The performers eventually shed their clothes, piece by piece, and throw the discarded articles into a pile in the center of the circle. In a postmodern spirit, this work both honors tradition and mocks it.

Chad Gadya has consistently been featured with illustrations in Haggadot and sometimes has been issued as a book of its own. Contemporary artists whose renderings are well known include Ben Shahn, El Lissitzky, Frank Stella (inspired by Lissitzky's work), and Maty Grunberg's *Bezalel Haggadah*. The song was poignantly reframed by the popular Israeli singer Chava Alberstein as a song of protest in 1989 during the first intifada. (Her work calls to mind Itik Manger's Yiddish poem in which two brothers "liberate" the goat from the prison of *Chad Gadya*, just as the ancient high priest once sent off a scapegoat into the wilderness on the Day of Atonement.) Alberstein's version begins with the traditional lyrics, sung to the joyous melody of the Italian *Alla fiera dell' est* popularized by Angelo Branduardi. In this English version, translated by Juliet I. Spitzer, we hear how Alberstein provokes the listener to ask how "the cycle of violence" as it now appears in the Middle East can be broken and how Israelis can find their own healing as neither victims nor aggressors.

Why are you singing this traditional song?
It's not yet spring and Passover's not here.

And what has changed for you? What has changed?
I have changed this year.
On all other nights I ask the four questions, but
    tonight I have one more:
How long will the cycle last?
How long will the cycle of horror last?
The chased and the chaser
The beaten and the beater
When will all this madness end?
I used to be a kid and a peaceful sheep
Today I am a tiger and a ravenous wolf.
I used to be a dove and I used to be a deer,
Today I don't know who I am anymore.
Deezvan abba beetray zuzay ...
And we start all over again.[30]

Originally banned by the Israeli government from the Israeli airwaves, it is now regularly broadcast on the radio as part of the Passover season repertoire. It received international exposure when it was used as the opening for Amos Gitai's 2005 film *Free Zone*, as the character played by Natalie Portman listens to the song for ten full minutes in a car as she cries for reasons unknown.

Why Have We Needed So Many Haggadot?

As this life of the Haggadah reaches its conclusion, I want to share the question that has fueled my investigations and reflect on how I am, for now, responding to it. Why has the Haggadah needed so much revision? I believe it is because the Haggadah holds within its DNA, so to speak, three imperfections.

The first imperfection is liturgical. As a set of prayers, rituals, and study texts that have accrued through the years, the Haggadah aims to focus prayerful energies, sustain concentration, transmit sacred narratives, and forge connections to the divine. But the unwieldly text it contains, despite the excellent intentions of generations of mostly unnamed authors, dissipates attention as much as it holds it. Further, the liturgy simply cannot replace the compelling earlier Passover practice, the mass national pilgrimage to the Temple in Jerusalem when the Israelites experienced what Durkheim refers to as collective effervescence, a group practice that generates "a kind of electricity that quickly transports them to an extraordinary degree of exaltation."[31] No Haggadah can orchestrate a family dining ritual that fully elicits the pilgrim's communitas. How could any liturgy compare with physically journeying up to Jerusalem among masses of people and the sound, smell, and taste of sacrificed lambs? True enough, the imaginative replacement for Passover at the Temple forged in the crucible of rabbinic Judaism has been standing in for so long that it is no longer experienced as having once been new or compensatory. The seder has become its own real thing with its own long past. Were all Jews not just well educated, but experts in mystical practice, this new liturgy evoking pilgrimage might be fully able to conjure up the steps, sounds, smells, sociality, and feeling of the more ancient embodied one. The Haggadah that eventually emerged as a promptbook for ritualizing and remembering would have been sufficient for spiritual virtuosos who could find storytelling, drinking wine, and pointing to a little piece of roasted bone on a plate at home to be transformative. But for regular folks, even the most engaging of narratives, comprehensible symbolic acts, and the pleasantness of a family feast cannot replace a complex visceral experience that included animal sacrifice to one singular God, in one particular holy place, followed by consumption, as a sign of piety. Perhaps this explains why so many Jews obsess about Passover preparations, spending weeks on ladders dusting the prisms of chandeliers, vacuuming crevices behind their dressers, and shaking out the pages of books for the leaven that is forbidden during the holiday. Can all the attentive focus on housework compensate for the ancient engaging spiritual experience? I don't think so.

Which brings us to a second imperfection. As pedagogical text, the Haggadah works for those who have studied the text beforehand in detail and have come to the table with a solid background in the Hebrew Bible, and better still, a facility in reading its commentaries and decoding rabbinical literature. That is to say, the Haggadah provides, for the best educated, illumination and a springboard for further study of the layers of commentary. It can offer those who have the most to learn happy memories of family fellowship and some Judaic content, but it leaves them with little edification and little incentive to learn more. Questions are asked in the Haggadah that are not answered. Answers are given to questions that have not been asked. The pedantry can overwhelm. Biblical narratives are referred to, but in such oblique and cryptic ways that it is hard to piece a coherent story together. Consider this passage in the Haggadah:

"Populous"—as it says, "I made your population like wildflowers, and you were populous and large, and you grew into a woman. Your breasts grew and your hair sprouted, yet you remained naked and bare." "I passed by you and I saw you wallowing in your blood. And I said to you, live in your blood. And I said to you, live in your blood."[32]

If you don't recognize these verses from Ezekiel (16:7, 6) that are used to describe God's relationship to the large nation of Hebrew slaves that had grown up in Egypt, then you are lost. And even if you do know the reference, you may still find yourself befuddled, hoping the next passages won't be as oblique.

Thus, even if the Haggadah has been translated, transliterated, personalized, illustrated, and embellished with commentary and fascinating tidbits—and perhaps as a consequence of too much elaborate and cumbersome paratextual material—there is insufficient accessible takeaway for those who are not erudite. The various flaws of the Haggadah as an evening's lesson plan are exacerbated by the fact that usually those leading the way through difficult materials are members of the household—that is, amateurs, not master Jewish teachers or ritual experts who know how to mine the material and explicate it in an engaging manner so it comes to life.

Finally, the third imperfection: the Haggadah poses an overwhelming theological challenge without providing satisfying resources to address it. The Haggadah invites a celebration of a rare joyous moment in the Jewish narrative, when God liberated the Hebrew slaves who cried out. But even in a celebratory state of mind, one struggles to understand why God appears to no longer hear the suffering of God's children or to provide salvation. Outside the Haggadah, Jewish texts provide multiple strategies for engaging with God's distance. It is told, for instance, that Jews brought terrible fates on themselves through their own sins, and further, that God is the very source of their destruction and exile. God regrets having to punish in this kind of way. Seeing Jerusalem in ruin, God laments: "Woe to me, that due to their sins I destroyed my house, burned my Temple and exiled them among the nations of the world."[33] What might those reciting the Haggadah in dire periods conclude when their own cries were not heeded? Were they not also worthy of being rescued as their ancestors enslaved in Egypt? What amount of prayer, study, and good deeds would it take for God to choose to intervene, once again, in history and provide salvation before the end of days? And if they were indeed worthy, and the period of penance had concluded, was God no longer able to intervene?

In his Haggadah commentary, *Zevach Pesach*, Abarbanel gave voice to the irony of celebrating Passover when he and his Jewish countrymen were being persecuted and sent into exile from Spain in 1492. He asked: "What benefit have we in the Diaspora today derived from the Exodus from Egypt? Isn't it possible that we would have been better off in Egypt than in our contemporary exile among Edom and Ishmael?" Abarbanel paraphrased the freed Israelites who complained to Moses during their desert wanderings, updating their lament for his own situation: "We would rather toil for Egypt than die in this wilderness of the nations, with its forced conversions and expulsions, where so many of us come to a bitter end, be it by sword, hunger, captivity, or worst of all, abandonment of faith."[34] For a desolate Abarbanel, it seemed that the story of Exodus foreshadowed a history of exile without end. Post-Holocaust theologians have posited a different response, saying it may no longer be supportable to maintain the idea of an all-powerful God, capable of rescue.

The Haggadah does not overtly engage with such matters. Instead, it frames remembering the liberation as a lesson in moral edification. "We are grateful for what God did for us once long ago in Egypt. Having been saved ourselves cultivates our empathy for those whom we see suffering now. We should act in God's image and attend to their needs." The lesson of gratitude translated into action is an excellent one, but it does not fully distract from the fact that matters of theodicy have been raised and have not been addressed in a satisfying way. (Indeed, is that even possible?)

These liturgical, pedagogical, and theological imperfections exist as the emperor's—that is, the Haggadah's invisible new clothes. One senses them but resists dwelling on them out of respect or nostalgia.

I wonder: are the Haggadah's imperfections, like wrinkles on the face of an elder, not flaws, but signs of a life sustained and characterized by centuries of generativity? Or does the Haggadah keep on living, as an imperfect form, because if it is fully repaired, it will cease being a received form that maintains meaningful ties between the present and the past?

I believe both these claims are valid. The Haggadah stays alive not because it has been preserved unchanged, but because it has been perpetually reimagined—five thousand times, six thousand times, with more to come. Or as

Yerushalmi wrote, "As these words are being written, one is confident that Jewish printers in far-flung places are already preparing other Haggadahs for local or foreign markets in anticipation of the Passover to come."[35]

And they are. But it is no longer just the printers in far-flung places who are busy. A Haggadah can be given life by just about anyone, even someone who is about to attend a seder for the very first time.

Haggadot will be created and read as long as the conventions for its usage remain in place. As a text meant to be recited at a dinner table overflowing with food and wine, the Haggadah works because it trains its celebrants to digest metaphors and experience them as spiritual facts. Song too—there needs to be singing, probably by those who are, by night's end, in good spirits. There must be conversation to rupture the recital, to challenge the status quo, and to make the evening personal and memorable. Take any of these elements away, remove conviviality and script it with less room for improvisation, and the Haggadah might never have become so beloved. Or remain so.

There will be Haggadot as long as there are Jewish children encouraged to ask their parents why the old story is still being retold, and why in such a fractured form? As long as Jewish pedagogy prefers questions over answers, rewards challenges, tolerates dissension, and assumes that minds of the young and old can accommodate multiple and contradictory answers, a Haggadah will sustain the conversation. (If this is hard to picture, watch Woody Allen's brilliant seder scene in *Crimes and Misdemeanors* or the racy, but still touching film *When Do We Eat*, which lifts its visual inspiration off the pages of the Szyk Haggadah.)

Haggadot will be created as long as Jews keep claiming that the traditional norms have been preserved even when changes clearly have been inserted over generations. The Haggadah's hallmark disjointedness and absence of literary unity preserve its being endlessly in process, stable in its instability, and always needing repair.

Who knows which present editions will fade into obscurity? So many have come and gone over the years. The most felicitous disappearances can be attributed to missions that have been accomplished. Think, for example, of Zionist Haggadot published in the first half of the twentieth century focused on the imperative of establishing a Jewish homeland. More recently, think of the Haggadot of the 1970s and 1980s that cast light on the plight of unfree Soviet Jews. And think of the commemorative Haggadah presented by the Israeli police to the parents of the kidnapped (and finally freed) soldier Gilad Shalit.

Traditional Haggadot, even without translations into the vernacular, will be used as long as there are Jews who believe they are commanded to perform the seder ritual in the way that it has been practiced for over a thousand years. For some, Haggadot will crescendo toward a dream of redemption, depicted as a return to Jerusalem, where the faithful will rebuild the Temple and be pilgrims once again who offer sacrifice. Others will conjure up yet-to-be-scripted messianic ages.

In years to come, even new technologies will enter the Haggadah. Wearing special glasses, one's text may reveal life-sized speaking holograms of virtual slaves in Egypt along with relatives who have passed on. A Haggadah portal may enable a *Chad Gadya* sing-along in all the world's languages. Reciting "let all who are hungry come eat" could, after the holiday, activate automatic contributions to food banks, send letters to elected officials, and maybe even irrigate crops. A Haggadah might come with a chip that Jewish parents can implant in the brains of their children guaranteeing they will fulfill the Passover commandment of imparting the Exodus story to their children. Once and for all.

"The need for new Haggadahs," said Jonathan Safran Foer in his musing on their unremitting evolution, "does not imply the failure of existing ones, but the struggle to engage everyone at the table in an ancient story in a time that is unlike any that has come before."[36] This holds true even for his own.

Imagine in your hands, as Foer suggests, an object claiming to be a Haggadah of the future. However curious it may be, you know that is a Haggadah. How so? Because it celebrates an old story of miraculous liberation. Even though the hope that divine human, or combined efforts will bring about a more complete liberation has gone unfulfilled for so very long, it keeps on hoping.

ACKNOWLEDGMENTS

I thank Fred Appel for creating this series and inviting me to write about the Haggadah, the book I am always most delighted to hold in my hands. So many scholars, private collectors, museum curators, librarians, and educators in America and Israel have been generous with their wisdom and materials, and I thank them all. I am especially grateful to Rabbi Lawrence Hoffman for the depth and generosity of his teachings. Thanks go also to my colleagues and research assistants—in particular, to Dr. Kelly Figueroa-Ray. Hats off to the many University of Virginia students who have studied the life of the Haggadah along with me and have created meaningful Haggadot of their own. Always, I thank my family: Peter, Julie, Yaob, Elizabeth, Taylor, and the grandchildren: Emma, Harry and Isaiah. Mims, of course, and all the Goldsteins.

My research and writing on the Haggadah were made possible by the generosity of the College of Arts and Sciences of the University of Virginia, the Virginia Seminar in Lived Theology, the Frankel Institute for Advanced Judaic Studies at the University of Michigan, and Repair the World.

Those wishing to deepen their study of the life of the Haggadah would do well to begin with: *Haggadah and History* by Yosef Hayim Yerushalmi; *The Origins of the Seder: The Passover Rite and Early Rabbinic Judaism* by Baruch Bokser; *My People's Passover Haggadah: Traditional Texts, Modern Commentaries* (vols. 1 and 2), edited by Lawrence A. Hoffman and David Arnow; *Beyond the Text* by Lawrence A. Hoffman; *The Schechter Haggadah: Art, History, and Commentary* by Joshua Kulp, with illuminations edited by David Golinkin; and the facsimile of the Washington Haggadah introduced by David Stern and Katrin Kogman-Appel. The Haggadah collection at the National Library of Israel is the largest in the world; one can access scanned texts from the early years of printing and from the kibbutzim. See: http://web.nli.org.il/sites/NLI/English/gallery/of-israel/haggadot/Pages/Introduction.aspx and http://web.nli.org.il/sites/NLI/English/gallery/of-israel/Pages/non-traditional-haggadot1.aspx. An excellent digitized collection of later printed Haggadot in many languages can be found at www.hebrewbooks.org/hagada.

The website titled "An Invitation to Piyut" offers digital recordings preserving much of the Haggadah's music that has been created by Jews of different lands and traditions, including those coming from Ashkenaz, Greece, Israel,

North America, Libya, Salonika, Tunisia, and various Hassidic sects. http://www.piyut.org.il/.

Finally, to make your own Haggadah with lots of assistance, you can turn to www.haggadot.com/, a free online platform originated by Los Angeles designer and artist Eileen Levinson.

Afikomen: Based on the Greek *epikomen* or *epikomion*, it has come to refer to a half-piece of matzah that is hidden and eaten at the conclusion of the seder's festive meal. Afterward, no other food is eaten.

Chad Gadya: Haggadah folk song, "An Only Goat."

Chametz: Leavened products forbidden on Passover.

Charoset: Fruity nut paste on the seder plate.

Dayenu: Haggadah prayer, "It would have been sufficient."

Echad Mi Yode'a: Haggadah folk song, "Who Knows One?"

Genizah: Repository for discarded sacred writing with Hebrew characters.

Haggadah: Literally, the telling. Plural: in Hebrew, *Haggadot*; in Yiddish, *Hagodes*.

Hallel: A selection of psalms included in Haggadah; also a part of the liturgy for festivals and the beginning of every month.

Hiddur mitzvah: Adding aesthetic enhancement to a commanded practice.

Kiddush: Blessing recited over wine.

Mah Nishtanah: The Haggadah's four questions asked by a child.

Maror: Bitter herbs on the seder plate.

Matzah: Unleavened Passover bread. Plural, *Matzot*.

Midrash: Oral and then written texts compiled between 200 and 1000 CE, which reflect rabbinic interactions with the Bible that are of both a legal (*halakha*) and a sermonic (*aggada*) nature.

Mishnah: Oral law set down in writing in the Land of Israel under Roman rule at the turn of the third century, and attributed to Rabbi Judah the Prince.

Mitzvah: Commandment. Plural, *mitzvot*.

Pesach: Passover.

Seder: Ordered Passover meal.

Sh'foch hamot'cha: Haggadah prayer, "Pour out Your wrath upon the nations who do not know You."

Simanei haseder shel pesach: Signs of the order of the Passover seder.

Talmud: Oral teaching compiled in Palestine and Babylonia in the fifth and sixth centuries, respectively.

Torah: This includes the Five Books of Moses, the Writings, and the Prophets. Torah can also refer to the Five Books of Moses alone or to all of Jewish teaching.

Tosefta: Supplementary rabbinic teachings compiled around 220 CE.

Yeshivot: Schools of Jewish learning.

INTRODUCTION. THE LIFE OF THE HAGGADAH

1. Bronislaw Malinowski, *Argonauts of the Western Pacific: An Account of Native Enterprise and Adventure in the Archipelagoes of Melanesian New Guinea*, Studies in Economics and Political Science 65 (London: Routledge and Kegan Paul, 1922), 4.

2. Tony Kushner, *Death and Taxes: Hydriotaphia and Other Plays* (New York: Theatre Communications Group, 1998), 256.

3. Lorraine Gershun, "Wrapping Up Passover," *Being Jewish in Hawaii* (blog), https://beingjewishinhawaii.com/2011/04/29/wrapping-up-passover/.

4. Jonathan Brown, "Rare Jewish Manuscript Found in Garage Expected to Fetch £500,000," *The Independent*, November 19, 2013, online edition, sec. Culture, www.independent.co.uk/arts-entertainment/books/news/rare-jewish-manuscript-found-in-garage-expected-to-fetch-500000-8947620.html.

5. "Rabbi Eliezer Brodt on Haggadah Shel Pesach: Reflections on the Past and Present," *The Seforim Blog: All about Seforim—New and Old, and Jewish Bibliography* (blog), http://seforim.blogspot.com/2007/03/rabbi-eliezer-brodt-on-haggadah-shel.html.

6. Yosef Hayim Yerushalmi, *Haggadah and History: A Panorama in Facsimile of Five Centuries of the Printed Haggadah* (Philadelphia: Jewish Publication Society of America, 1975), 13–14.

7. Edward Rothstein, "Put Yourself in the Story of Passover: The Washington Haggadah at Metropolitan Museum of Art," *New York Times*, online edition, sec. Art and Design, Critic's Notebook, www.nytimes.com/2011/04/18/arts/design/the-washington-haggadah-at-metropolitan-museum-of-art.html.

8. Jacob Ari Labendz, "Passover Post-Peoplehood," *Lion-Swan's Way* (blog), https://labendz.wordpress.com/2013/03/18/passover-post-peoplehood/.

CHAPTER 1. HOW THE HAGGADAH CAME TO BE

1. Jews refer to the Bible as the Torah. This includes the Five Books of Moses, the Writings, and the Prophets. Torah can also refer to just the Five Books of Moses or to all of Jewish teaching.

2. Clearly, reading the Hebrew Bible in this way is not consistent with scientific scholarly understandings of how and when the various texts emerged.

3. Specifically: Exodus 12–13; Leviticus 23:4–8; Numbers 9:1–14, 28:16–25; Deuteronomy 16:1–8, 26:1–10; Joshua 5:10–12; I Kings 9:25; II Kings 21–23; II Chronicles 8:12–13, 30; 35:1–19; and Ezra 6:19–22.

4. David Stern, introduction to the *Washington Haggadah*, trans. David Stern (Cambridge, MA: Belknap Press of Harvard University Press, 2011), 4.

5. This term for spiritual kinship among Jews is eventually referred to as *Clal Yisrael*, the community of Israel.

6. Victor Turner, *Dramas, Fields, and Metaphors: Symbolic Action in Human Society* (Ithaca, NY: Cornell University Press, 1974), 273–74. Edith Turner, *Communitas: The Anthropology of Collective Joy* (New York: Palgrave Macmillan, 2012).

7. Lawrence A. Hoffman, "The Passover Meal in Jewish Tradition," in *Passover and Easter: Origin and History to Modern Times*, ed. Paul F. Bradshaw and Lawrence A. Hoffman, Two Liturgical Traditions 5 (Notre Dame, IN: University of Notre Dame Press, 1999), 15–18.

8. Judith Hauptman, "Does the Tosefta Precede with Mishnah: Halakhah, Aggada, and Narrative Coherence," *Judaism* 50, no. 2 (Spring 2001): 224–40; Judith Hauptman, "How Old Is the Haggadah?," *Judaism* 51, no. 1 (Winter 2002): 5–18.

9. The passages from the Mishnah and Tosefta are available in English translation in Joshua Kulp, trans., *The Schechter Haggadah: Art, History, and Commentary* (Jerusalem: Schechter Institute of Jewish Studies, 2009), 281–83.

10. Michael Walzer, *Exodus and Revolution* (New York: Basic Books, 1985), 88.

11. Jonathan Klawans, "Was Jesus' Last Supper a Seder?," *Bible Review* 17, no. 5 (2001): 29–30; see also Paul F. Bradshaw and Lawrence A. Hoffman, eds., *Passover and Easter*, vols. 5 and 6, Two Liturgical Traditions (Notre Dame, IN: University of Notre Dame Press, 1999); Jonathan Brumberg-Kraus, "'Not by Bread Alone . . .': The Ritualization of Food and Table Talk in the Passover Seder and in the Last Supper," *Semeia-Missoula*, no. 86 (1999): 165–92; and Israel Yuval, "Easter and Passover as Early Jewish-Christian Dialogue," in *Passover and Easter: Origin and History to Modern Times*, ed. Paul Bradshaw and Lawrence A. Hoffman, vol. 5, Two Liturgical Traditions (Notre Dame, IN: University of Notre Dame Press, 1999), 98–124.

12. Joshua Kulp writes: "Scholars will certainly continue to debate the interrelation between developing Christian and Jewish ritual for Passover eve, and the veracity of the different accounts of Jesus' last meal." Found in "The Origins of the Seder and Haggadah," *Currents in Biblical Research* 4, no. 1 (2005): 109–34.

13. David Berger, "Passover and Shavuot," Discussion Response, *H-Judaic Discussion: H-Net Humanities and Social Sciences Online*, http://h-net.msu.edu/cgi-bin/logbrowse.pl?trx.

14. B. Talmud Pesachim 116b.

15. J. A. Joel, "Passover—A Reminiscence of the War," *Jewish Messenger*, April 1866.

16. These are the biblical passages: Exodus 12:26–27, 13:3, 14–15, and Deuteronomy 6:20, 20–25. It is possible that the theme of fours in the Haggadah (four questions, four children, four cups of wine) is linked to the four relevant biblical passages.

17. Menachem M. Kasher, ed., *Israel Passover Haggadah* (New York: Shengold, 1983), 67.

CHAPTER 2. ON BECOMING A BOOK

1. For lively accounts, see Janet Martin Soskice, *The Sisters of Sinai: How Two Lady Adventurers Discovered the Hidden Gospels* (New York: Alfred A. Knopf, 2009); and Adina Hoffman and Peter Cole, *Sacred Trash: The Lost and Found World of the Cairo Geniza*, Jewish Encounters (New York: Schocken Books, 2011).

2. Lawrence A. Hoffman and David Arnow, eds., *My People's Passover Haggadah: Traditional Texts, Modern Commentaries*, vol. 2 (Woodstock, VT: Jewish Lights Publishing, 2008), 235; see also David Stern, "The Dropsie Haggadah," in *Breaking New Ground: Scholars and Scholarship at the Center for Advance Judaic Studies (1993–2004)* (Philadelphia: Center for Advanced Judaic Studies, University of Pennsylvania, 2004), 76–77.

3. A visual demonstration of how the Haggadah is constructed from sources of different eras, from biblical to contemporary, was created by Jacob Freedman: *Polychrome Historical Haggadah for Passover* (Springfield, MA: Jacob Freedman Liturgy Research Foundation, 1974). While its reliability has been challenged, it has nonetheless become a collector's item.

4. Note that not all the rituals are included, such as saying a blessing for drinking three of the four cups of wine. Presumably this was because those steps were considered so self-evident that instruction was not required.

5. The noted early commentators include Rashi (Shlomo Itzhaki, eleventh–twelfth centuries); his grandson Rabbenu Tam (Jacob ben Meir, twelfth century); Or Zarua (Isaac Ben Moses, twelfth–thirteenth centuries); Rabbi Meir of Rothernberg (thirteenth century); Orchot Chayim (Aaron ben Jacob Hakohen, thirteenth–fourteenth centuries); Ritba (Yom Tov Ishbili, fourteenth century); David ben Joseph Abudarham (fourteenth century); and Rashbetz Rabbi Shimon ben Tzemach (fourteenth–fifteenth centuries).

6. Moses Maimonides, *The Code of Maimonides, Book Three: The Book of Seasons*, trans. Solomon Gandz and Hyman Klein,

Yale Judaica Series vol. 14 (New Haven, CT: Yale University Press, 1961), 353.

7. Maimonides, 14:350.

8. Maimonides, 14:359.

9. Cecil Roth, "Birds' Heads and Graven Images," *Commentary* 47, no. 6 (June 1969): 80–83.

10. Marc Michael Epstein, *The Medieval Haggadah: Art, Narrative, and Religious Imagination* (New Haven, CT: Yale University Press, 2011), 7.

11. Marc Michael Epstein, "Illustrating History and Illuminating Identity in the Art of the Passover Haggadah," in *Judaism in Practice: From the Middle Ages through the Early Modern Period*, ed. Lawrence Fine (Princeton, NJ: Princeton University Press, 2001), 299–300.

12. The Birds' Head Haggadah has been reproduced and elaborated on as a popular pop-up and pull-tab book for children: *The Koren Birds' Head Haggada: A Hebrew/English Pop-Up Passover Haggada*, bilingual edition (Jerusalem: Koren Publishers, 2008).

13. Epstein, *Medieval Haggadah*, 57.

14. A full-color image of the page (f. 31b) from the Sarajevo Haggadah I discuss here can be found at www.talmud.de/sarajevo/. All of the images can be found in this two-volume facsimile and study by Shalom Sabar: *Sarajevo Haggadah: History and Art* (Sarajevo: National Museum of Bosnia and Herzegovina, 2018).

15. Eva Frojmovic, "Messianic Politics in RE-Christianized Spain," in *Imagining the Self, Imagining the Other: Visual Representation and Jewish-Christian Dynamics in the Middle Ages and Early Modern Period*, ed. Eva Frojmovic (Leiden: Brill, 2002), 108.

16. See Katrin Kogman-Appel, *Illuminated Haggadot from Medieval Spain: Biblical Imagery and the Passover Holiday* (University Park: Pennsylvania State University Press, 2006).

17. Edward Serotta, "Searching for Hope: The Sarajevo Hagaddah," *Nightline*, ABC News, 1996.

18. Geraldine Brooks, *People of the Book: A Novel* (New York: Viking, 2008).

19. Brooks, *People of the Book*, 195.

20. Douglas Perry, "Geraldine Brooks' Faith amid Catastrophe," *OregonLive.Com, The Oregonian*, January 14, 2009, online edition, sec. Bookmarks, http://blog.oregonlive.com/books/2009/01/geraldine_brooks_faith_amid_ca.html.

21. David Stern, trans., *The Washington Haggadah* (Cambridge, MA: Belknap Press of Harvard University Press, 2011), f. 34v, p. 155.

22. Sephardic and Yemenite Haggadot presented a more concise assemblage of Psalm-based verses of vengeance; the Ashkenazic versions were lengthier.

CHAPTER 3. THE PRINTED HAGGADAH AND ITS ENDURING CONVENTIONS

1. Yosef Hayim Yerushalmi, *Haggadah and History: A Panorama in Facsimile of Five Centuries of the Printed Haggadah* (Philadelphia: Jewish Publication Society of America, 1975), 23–24.

2. Yerushalmi, *Haggadah and History*, plate 59.

3. His name is also spelled as Abravanel.

4. I Chronicles 16:23–24, JPS translation.

5. Carol B. Balin offers the detailed story in "Good to the Last Drop: The Proliferation of the Maxwell House Haggadah," in *My People's Passover Haggadah: Traditional Texts, Modern Commentaries*, vol. 1, ed. Lawrence A. Hoffman and David Arnow (Woodstock, VT: Jewish Lights, 2008), 85–90.

6. Why is this night different from all other nights?

7. Mira Friedman, "Transplanted Illustrations in Jewish Printed Books," *Jewish Art* 4 (1988): 44–55.

8. Jonathan Safran Foer, "Why a Haggadah?," *New York Times*, April 1, 2012, sec. Sunday Review, Opinion. In Waldman, *The Koren Ethiopian Haggada: Journey to Freedom*, trans. Binyamin Shalom (Jerusalem: Koren Publishers, 2011), the copyright page does its best to fend off poaching. It reads: "Considerable research and expense has gone into the creation of this Haggada, and unauthorized

copying may be considered *geneivat daʾat* as well as breach of Copyright law." *Geneivat daʾat* is a rabbinical ethical precept, which is used in contemporary parlance to refer to failing to cite sources.

9. The earliest versions of his published commentary come from Venice in 1545; Cremona in 1557; Riva di Trento in 1561; Kraków in 1569; Prague in 1590; and Bistrowitz, Poland, in 1592; there are over a hundred more.

10. Shlomo Fox, ed., *Abarbanel Haggadah: The Passover Haggadah with the Commentary of Don Isaac Abarbanel*, ArtScroll Mesorah Series (Brooklyn, NY: Mesorah Publications, 1996), 28, 30, and 41.

11. Many translations of the Haggadah into Amharic have been produced in Israel, including a fancy Koren version that is promoted as a great wedding gift idea (unclear if it is meant for Ethiopian Jews in Israel or for collectors).

12. Waldman, *Koren Ethiopian Haggada*, 11.

13. Alexander Alexander, trans., *Haggadah of 1770*, found in: Yerushalmi, *Haggadah and History*, plate 74.

14. Alexander Alexander, trans., *Haggadah of 1770*, 2nd ed. (London: Levy Alexander, 1787), plate 6.

15. Jonathan Sacks, *Rabbi Jonathan Sacks's Haggadah: Hebrew and English Text with New Essays and Commentary* (New York: Continuum, 2006), 10.

CHAPTER 4. TWENTIETH-CENTURY VARIATIONS

1. Reform Jews, worldwide, hold one seder on the first night of the holiday. Israeli Jews observe this practice.

2. Adolf Guttmacher and William Rosenau, eds., *Year Book of the Central Conference of American Rabbis*, vol. 14 (Baltimore: Lord Baltimore Press, 1904), 84.

3. Central Conference of American Rabbis, ed., *The Union Haggadah* (Cincinnati: Bloch Publishing, 1907), 8–9.

4. Guttmacher and Rosenau, *Year Book of the Central Conference of American Rabbis*, 14:85.

5. Central Conference of American Rabbis, *Union Haggadah*, 7.

6. Central Conference of American Rabbis, *Union Haggadah*, 5.

7. Marcus Jastrow, *Family Service for the Eve of Passover* (Philadelphia, 1891), n. 4, p. 10.

8. Herbert Bronstein, ed., *A Passover Haggadah: The New Union Haggadah* (New York: Central Conference of American Rabbis, 1974), 5–6.

9. B. Talmud Sanhedrin 39b.

10. Bronstein, *New Union Haggadah*, 49.

11. Bronstein, *New Union Haggadah*, 93.

12. M. Altshuler's 1927 "Hagode far gloyber un apikorsem" (Haggadah for Believers and Heretics) was a Yiddish parody of the Haggadah, written in the USSR, which pressed for the abolition not just of Passover but of all Jewish religion.

13. Muky Tsur, "Pesach in the Land of Israel: Kibbutz Haggadot," *Israel Studies* 12, no. 2 (2007).

14. Mordechai Amitay, *Emek, Emek, Merhavia*, Sifriat-Poal'im and Ha-Shomer Ha'Tzair (1945), 233, cited in Avshalom Reich, "Changes and Developments in the Passover Haggadot of the Kibbutz Movement" (PhD diss., University of Texas, 1972), 7.

15. The National Library of Israel has an excellent collection of Kibbutz Haggadot; this online exhibit represents but a sampling: http://web.nli.org.il/sites/NLI/English/gallery/of-israel/passover/Pages/kibbutz.aspx.

16. Galia Bar Or, "Art Museums in Kibbutzim and the Museum of Art Ein Harod," Museum of Art, Ein Harod, accessed January 20, 2014, www.museumeinharod.org.il/english/about/articles/art_museums_in_kibbutzim.html.

17. *Haggadah Shel Pesach* (Ha-Kibbutz Ha-Artzi, 1964) in Shalom Lilker, *Kibbutz Judaism: A New Tradition in the Making* (New York: Herzl Press, 1982), 178.

18. Yosef Hayim Yerushalmi, *Haggadah and History: A Panorama in Facsimile of Five Centuries of the Printed Haggadah* (Philadelphia: Jewish Publication Society of America, 1975), plate 166.

19. Yerushalmi, *Haggadah and History*, plate 175.

20. In Israel, national holidays were established to mark (1) the Holocaust and the heroes of Jewish resistance on Yom hazikaron lashoah ve-lag'vurah, better known as Yom Hashoah, and in English as Holocaust Remembrance Day (1953); (2) the memorial day for soldiers, Yom Hazikaron, the Day of Remembrance for the Fallen Soldiers of Israel and Victims of Terrorism (established in stages, in 1953 and 1961); and set to be observed on the following day, (3) Yom Haatzmaut, Israel Independence Day (1948).

21. Words of *Tsint on di licht* (Light the Candles) by Solomon Frug, music by Eugene Malek. Neil W. Levin, "Liner Notes | Third Seder of the Arbeter Ring," Digital Archive, Milken Archive of Jewish Music, www.milkenarchive.org/works/view/540#/works/lyrics/540. Here, in this archive, one can hear a reconstruction of third seder songs.

22. Jack Wertheimer, "Kaplan vs. 'the Great Do-Nothings': The Inconclusive Battle over The New Haggadah," *Conservative Judaism* 45 (1993): 29–30, 31, 26.

23. Rachel Anne Rabinowicz, ed., *Passover Haggadah: The Feast of Freedom* (New York: Rabbinical Assembly, 1982), 6.

CHAPTER 5. HAGGADOT OF DARKNESS

1. Cited in Siegfried Guggenheim, *Rudolf Koch: His Work and the Offenbach Workshop* (Woodstock, VT: William Edwin Rudge, 1947), 32.

2. "Haggadot from Leo Baeck Institute Collections," *Highlights, Leo Baeck Institute Website* (blog), https://old.lbi.org/2014/04/three-haggadot-from-lbi-collections/. Leo Baeck Institute maintains an online digitized Siegfried Guggenheim archival collection. Brünn is called Brno today; it is in the Czech Republic.

3. Cokie Roberts and Steven V. Roberts, *Our Haggadah: Uniting Traditions for Interfaith Families* (New York: Harper-Collins, 2011), xxviii.

4. Roberts and Roberts, *Our Haggadah*, 65.

5. Siegfried Guggenheim, "Siegfried Guggenheim Collection, 1791–1969, Box 2, Folder 23: 'Drafts and Corrections'" (Internet Archive, Leo Baeck Institute Archive, 2010), 1237, https://archive.org/details/siegfriedguggenheim05reel05.

6. Guggenheim, "Siegfried Guggenheim Collection," 1057.

7. Arthur Szyk's *The Szyk Haggadah: Freedom Illuminated*, trans. Byron L. Sherwin (New York: Abrams, 2010), is a facsimile that reproduces all the images of this Haggadah in full color.

8. The testimony of Fay P. in Liora Gubkin, *You Shall Tell Your Children: Holocaust Memory in American Passover Ritual* (New Brunswick, NJ: Rutgers University Press, 2007), 47–48.

9. Yaffa Eliach, *Hasidic Tales of the Holocaust* (New York: Oxford University Press, 1982), 17–18.

10. Israel I. Cohen, *Destined to Survive: Uplifting Stories from the Worst of Times* (Brooklyn, NY: Mesorah Publications, 2001), 214–15.

11. Gubkin, *You Shall Tell Your Children*, 45.

12. The Center for Holocaust and Humanity Education, "Inspirations from the Jewish Experience: Passover," www.holocaustandhumanity.org/education/online-exhibits/faith/passover/. Museum curators routinely wrestle with the ethical implications of installing Holocaust artifacts such as Haggadot and Torah scrolls into their collections. There is always the risk, however unintentional, of disrespect. By exalting material artifacts of the Holocaust era by attending to the sweetness of the object and the comfort it provided—is one not domesticating the horror? See Vanessa L. Ochs, *Inventing Jewish Ritual* (Philadelphia: Jewish Publication Society, 2007), 187–209.

13. A facsimile edition of the handwritten Haggadah was published as, Belah Guterman, No'omi Morgenshtern, and Aryeh Ludvig Tsukerman, eds., *The Gurs Haggadah: Passover in Perdition* (Jerusalem: Yad Vashem and Devorah Publishing, 2003).

14. See "IJA #2921" (Iraqi Jewish Archive), www.ija.archives.gov/content/2921; see also "Retrieving Baghdad's Vanished Jewish Past | Photographic Slideshow," *Washington Post*, August 13, 2013, online edition, www.washingtonpost.com/local/retrieving

-baghdads-vanished-jewish-past/2013/08/12/941bc8a2-0384-11e3
-88d6-d5795fab4637_gallery.html.

15. Yosef Dov Sheinson, *A Survivors' Haggadah*, ed. Saul
Touster (Philadelphia: Jewish Publication Society, 2000), 25.

16. Sheinson, *A Survivors' Haggadah*, 63.

17. Issued 1953 by Seder Ritual Committee, 15 E. Eighty-
Fourth Street, New York, New York.

18. Rachel Anne Rabinowicz, ed., *Passover Haggadah: The
Feast of Freedom* (New York: Rabbinical Assembly, 1982), 9.

19. Gubkin, *You Shall Tell Your Children*.

20. Irving Greenberg, *Guide to Passover* (New York: National
Jewish Center for Learning and Leadership, 1976), 12–13.

21. Greenberg, *Guide to Passover*, 15.

22. The National Jewish Center for Learning and Leadership, "Perspectives on the Holocaust," National Jewish Center for
Learning and Leadership, April 1986, 21.

23. Elie Wiesel, *Hagadah shel pesah = A Passover Haggadah: As Commented upon by Elie Wiesel and Illustrated by Mark
Podwal*, ed. Marion Wiesel (New York: Simon and Schuster,
1993), 79.

24. Gubkin, *You Shall Tell Your Children*, 1.

25. Mishael Zion and Noam Zion, *A Night to Remember: The
Haggadah of Contemporary Voices* (Jerusalem: Zion Holiday Publications, 2007).

26. Alan S. Yoffie, *Sharing the Journey: The Haggadah for the
Contemporary Family*, ed. Mary L. Zamore (New York: CCAR
Press, 2012), 28.

27. Yoffie, *Sharing the Journey*, 28.

CHAPTER 6. THE HAGGADAH OF THE MOMENT

1. Jay Michaelson, "'Tis the Season for New Haggadot:
Comparing the Best and Biggest Names for Passover," *Jewish Daily
Forward*, online edition, sec. Arts & Culture, http://forward.com
/articles/153440/tis-the-season-for-new-haggadot/.

2. To secure a copy of this Haggadah, one needed to purchase a Maxwell House product on the Amazon Prime website. Full disclosure: In the name of research, I did.

3. Michael Rubiner, "The Two-Minute Haggadah: A Passover Service for the Impatient," *Slate*, www.slate.com/articles/news_and _politics/low_concept/2006/04/the_twominute_haggadah.html.

4. They are Barbara Wolff, Rudy Wolff, Izzy Pludwinski, and Karen Gorst.

5. Videos include: *The Bronfman Haggadah Book Trailer*, 2013, www.youtube.com/watch?v=tvQpG51ssWw&feature= youtube_gdata_player; *Daniel and Joanna S. Rose Haggadah: An Illuminated Haggadah for the 21st Century*, http://vimeopro .com/user1305805/an-illuminated-haggadah/video/61997636; and *HAGGADAH—Tamar Messer*, 2013, www.youtube.com /watch?v=2bkbinX-_lA&feature=youtube_gdata_player.

6. Another Haggadah that has been kept in captivity, so to speak, is the original 2005 *Aachen Passover Haggadah* by the Russian-born Israeli artist Zoya Cherkassky. It was displayed at galleries in London and Tel Aviv, and then it entered the collection of Jerusalem's Israel Museum.

7. Jan Hoffman, "Make Your Own Tradition: Redefining Seders for Today," *New York Times*, April 10, 1998, online edition, sec. Archives, www.nytimes.com/1998/04/10/nyregion/make -your-own-tradition-redefining-seders-for-today.html.

8. Michael Medved, "The Preposterous Politics of Passover," *Commentary*, April 1, 2011, www.commentarymagazine.com/article /the-preposterous-politics-of-passover/.

9. Published first in *RAMPARTS* magazine in 1969, and in Rabbi Arthur Waskow, *The Freedom Seder: A New Haggadah for Passover* (New York: Holt, Rinehart, Winston; Washington, DC: Micah Press, 1970), https://theshalomcenter.org/sites/default /files/Freedom_Seder_1970A.pdf.

10. Arthur Waskow, "Arrested!—Palms, Matzah, the Globe, and the White House," *The Shalom Center* (blog), https:// theshalomcenter.org/arrested-palms-matzah-globe-and-white -house.

11. Adina Gerver, ed., *Food and Justice Haggadah Supplement* (New York: Uri L'Tzedek, 2011), 23.

12. Elana Fox and Jewish Council for Public Affairs staff, eds., *Hunger Seder* (New York: Jewish Council for Public Affairs, 2011), www.jewishpublicaffairs.org/Hagaddah/HungerSederHagaddah.pdf.

13. The Seattle version of *The Rice Paper Haggadah* was published in a revised version along with two other Haggadot in *The Shalom Seders: Three Haggadahs* (New York: Adama Books, 1984).

14. This excerpt of *The Rice Paper Haggadah* is included in "This Year in Brooklyn: A Seder to Commemorate Ourselves," *Off Our Backs* 3, no. 8 (May 31, 1973), a first-person account by Bobbie Spalter-Roth.

15. According to Nomi Nimrod, in the film by Lilly Rivlin, *Esther Broner: A Weave of Women*, 2013; Broner and Nimrod's Haggadah was revised and included in Broner's 1993 book: *The Telling: The Story of a Group of Jewish Women Who Journey to Community through Spirituality and Ceremony* (San Francisco: HarperSanFrancisco, 1993); and as a freestanding book: E. M. Broner and Naomi Nimrod, *The Women's Haggadah* (San Francisco: HarperSanFrancisco, 1994).

16. A final version was edited by Tamara Cohen: *The Journey Continues: The Ma'yan Passover Haggadah* (New York: Ma'yan, The Jewish Women's Project of the JCC on the Upper West Side, 2006). Nearly 40,000 copies of Ma'yan Haggadot were sold, and a Russian translation was used in women's seders held in the former Soviet Union.

17. Broner and Nimrod, *The Women's Haggadah*, 31.

18. September 13, 2011, personal correspondence with Rabbi Rachel Barenblat, printed with permission. Her Haggadah called *The Velveteen Rabbi's Haggadah for Pesach*, version 8, 2015, https://velveteenrabbi.files.wordpress.com/2015/02/vrhaggadah6.pdf.

19. Rabbi Geela Rayzel Raphael, "Five Interfaith Passover Readings You Can Add to Your Haggadah," in *Passover in Interfaith Families: Three Essays from InterfaithFamily.com, with*

Discussion Guide, Tips, Recommended Resources, and Activities for Children, www.interfaithfamily.com/files/pdf/passover ininterfaithfamilies.pdf.

20. Fair Trade Judaica, "Bean of Affliction: Chocolate, Child Labor, and Fair Trade Haggadah Supplement," 2012, http://fairtradejudaica.org/wp-content/uploads/2012/03/Haggadah Supplement2012.pdf.

21. Steve Lipman, "The Tomato Finds Its Place on the Seder Plate," *New York Jewish Week*, March 27, 2012, www.thejewishweek .com/special_sections/special_holiday_issues/tomato_finds_its _place_seder_plate.

22. Progressive Jewish Alliance, "Food Desert Plate—Beitzah," accessed March 17, 2014, http://haggadot.com/clip/food-desert -plate-beitzah.

23. Roberta Kalechofsky, *Haggadah for the Liberated Lamb* (Marblehead, MA: Micah Publications, 1988).

24. Gays, Lesbians, Bi-, and Transgendered individuals. All quotes from the Haggadah can be found at JQ International, "GLBT Haggadah," Make Your Own Passover Haggadah | Haggadot.com, 2008, www.haggadot.com/haggadah/jq -international-glbt-haggadah.

25. HIAS, "Ten Plagues Facing Refugees in the U.S. and Worldwide from 'HIAS Seder Supplement,'" Make Your Own Passover Haggadah | Haggadot.com, www.haggadot.com/clip/ten -plagues-facing-refugees-us-and-worldwide.

26. Jacob Alperin-Sheriff, "Republican—Who Knows One?," Make Your Own Passover Haggadah | Haggadot.com, www .haggadot.com/clip/republican-who-knows-one.

27. *The Sayder* was included in one of the first Haggadah "apps" for tablets and smartphones: *The Haggadah App* by Melcher Media.

28. Amichai Lau-Lavie, *Sayder: Four New Questions, One Real Conversation* (The Sayder Inc., 2012). Lau-Lavie created a version in Hebrew, "Kushiyot Chadashot" (New Questions), designed so it could be used as a placemat.

29. The Israel composer Oded Zehavi, who set the poet Chaim Nachman Bialik's version of *Chad Gadya* to music, suggested this contrast to me.

30. Juliet I. Spitzer's translation is an adaptation of Richard Silverstein's English translation of Chava Alberstein's *Chad Gadya*. Permission granted by Juliet I. Spitzer to use her translation.

31. Émile Durkheim, *The Elementary Forms of Religious Life*, trans. Carol Cosman (Oxford: Oxford University Press, 2001), 162.

32. Lawrence A. Hoffman and David Arnow, eds., *My People's Passover Haggadah: Traditional Texts, Modern Commentaries*, vol. 2 (Woodstock, VT: Jewish Lights Publishing, 2008), 1.

33. B. Talmud Brachot 3a.

34. Shlomo Fox, ed., *Abarbanel Haggadah: The Passover Haggadah with the Commentary of Don Isaac Abarbanel*, ArtScroll Mesorah Series (Brooklyn, NY: Mesorah Publications, 1996), 34.

35. Yosef Hayim Yerushalmi, *Haggadah and History: A Panorama in Facsimile of Five Centuries of the Printed Haggadah* (Philadelphia: Jewish Publication Society of America, 1975), 14.

36. Jonathan Safran Foer, "Why a Haggadah?," *New York Times*, April 1, 2012, sec. Sunday Review, Opinion, v–vi.

A page number in italics refers to an illustration.

Aaron, 20, 50, 71; image in 1695
    Amsterdam Haggadah, *80*;
    image in King James Bible, *79*
Abarbanel, Isaac, 71, 82, 169–70
Abaye, 35–36
Abraham, 19, 22, 32, 39
Abzug, Bella, 151
Adler, Miklós, 128
afikomen, 34, 39, 43; in Birds'
    Head Haggadah, 50; in
    Tosefta ceremony, 26
Akiva (Talmudic sage), 33
Alberstein, Chava, 164–65
Alexander, A., 87–88
Allen, Woody, 171
Altmann, Maria, 53
American Jewish Congress,
    memorial liturgy for Holo-
    caust victims, 130–32, 133
Amram Gaon, 40, 41
Amsterdam Haggadah of 1695:
    borrowed images in, 75–77,
    79, *80*; commentary in mar-
    gins of, 82–83; copper en-
    graved images in, 70, 71, *77*,
    114; in Durchslag collection,
2; explanations in, 86; with
    foldout map of Israel in bibli-
    cal times, 71; four sons illus-
    trated in, *77*; influence on
    subsequent printed editions,
    67, 69–70; Passover songs in-
    cluded in, 161; promotional
    material in, 70–71; transla-
    tions included in, 84–85
Amsterdam Haggadah of 1712,
    2, 67, 79
Angel, Marc C., 141
Angel of Death: lamb's blood as
    sign for, 20; repurposed illus-
    tration of, as Esther, 76–77
Ani Ma'amin (I Believe), 131, 135
The Animated Haggadah, 143
Ansbacher, Leo, 125
Arbeter Ring (Workmen's
    Circle), 105, 106–7
Ari (Isaac Luria Ashkenazi), 82
artichokes, welcoming inter-
    faith families, 154
artists of recent versions, 14,
    143–44; rendering *Chad
    Gadya* (An Only Goat), 164

ArtScroll Haggadah, 111–12
ArtScroll Mesorah, 111
artwork of Haggadot: of
    Arthur Szyk, 119–22, *120*;
    Chad Gadya (An Only
    Goat) rendered in, 164; in
    Conservative Haggadah of
    1982, 110; copper engravings
    in, 70, 71, 76, 114; in kibbut-
    zim, 102; medieval introduc-
    tion of visual elements, 46–
    47; in Offenbach Haggadah
    of 1920s, 113–15; in Offen-
    bach of 1722, 114; paper cut-
    ting and microcalligraphy,
    143; of Podwal in 2012 Re-
    form Haggadah, 138; of Sieg-
    mund Forst in 1951 Abraham
    Regelson Haggadah, 111; in
    today's market, 14, 143–44;
    Union Haggadot of Reform
    movement and, 94, 96, 97;
    woodcuts in, 68, 69, 114, *115*,
    128. *See also* illuminated
    Haggadot
Asher Anshel ben Eliezer
    Chazan, 71
Ashkenazi Jews: English trans-
    lation for, 87; Haggadot with
    Yiddish instructions for, 84–
    85; owning a Haggadah by
    fifteenth century, 46; region
    represented by, 44
Atar, Hayim, 102
Azulai, Haim Yosef David
    (Chida), 82

ba'al haseder, 33
Babylonian Haggadah tradition,
    41, 42, 44
Barenblat, Rachel, 152–53
Baskin, Leonard, 97
Batsheva Ensemble, 163
Benedikt family, 53
Bene Israel Jews of India, 16, 85
Berger, David, 32
Berkowitz, Matt, 143
Beta YISRAEL, 85–86
Bet Ha-Shitah Haggadah, 104
Bezalel Haggadah, 164
Bialik, Hayim Nachman, 97, 104
Bibatz, Samson, 53
Bible: King James Bible of 1611,
    79, *79*; sources of Passover
    rituals in, 19–23. See also II
    Chronicles; Deuteronomy;
    Exodus; Esther; Genesis;
    Numbers; Song of Songs
bibliographies of Haggadot, 15
Birds' Head Haggadah, 49–54, *51*
Birnbaum Haggadah, 110
bitter herbs: artist's gendered
    joke about, 62; in biblical
    book of Exodus, 20; early
    decorative motifs represent-
    ing, 47; in Elie Wiesel's
    Haggadah, 135–36; Mai-
    monides on rules of, 44; in
    new practices after destruc-
    tion of Second Temple, 24;
    as reminders of Egyptians,
    30; in rituals of Holocaust
    Remembrance Day, 136;

sandwich of charoset and, 8,
43, 51, 135–36; in Sheinson's
Haggadah for Holocaust survivors, 129; social justice supplement using, 148; in steps
of seder, 8, 9, 43. See also
maror

blessings: for foods in Dropsie
Haggadah, 41; over matzah,
8, 43, 55; recast as statements
in Arbeter Ring Haggadah,
107; recited from Haggadah
for other festivals, 46; in
steps of seder, 8, 43; studied
by rabbis of the Talmud, 34

blind rabbis, 33

Bonaventura de la Nay, 113–14

borrowed images, 75–81; from
Christian sources, 75–76,
78–79; in Haggadot for private use, 80–81

Boussidan, Ya'akov, 143

Branduardi, Angelo, 164

Broner, E. M., 151, 152

Bronstein, Herbert, 97

Brooks, Geraldine, 59–60

Buber, Martin, 97

Burning the Days (Salter), 4

cantillation, traditions of, 11

Cantor, Aviva, 151

Chad Gadya (An Only Goat),
161, 162, 164–65, 172

Chakovsky, Bria, 150

charoset: in Elie Wiesel's
Haggadah, 136; in home

ceremony of Tosefta, 26; in
illuminated Haggadot, 51; as
mitzvah, 35–37; orange-
flavored in GLBT Haggadah,
156; sandwich of bitter herbs
and, 8, 43, 51, 135–36; in Sarajevo Haggadah, 54; in steps
of seder, 8, 9; Talmudic
debate on, 35–37

Cherkassy, Zoya, 14, 192n6

Chesler, Phyllis, 151

Chida (Haim Yosef David
Azulai), 82

chocolate on seder plate, 154

Christian sources of imagery:
borrowed images, 75–76,
78–79; illuminating prac-
tices, 48, 54

II Chronicles, biblical book of, 23

circumcision, 22

CLAL (National Jewish Center
for Learning and Leadership),
134

Clal Yisrael, 182n5

Cleaver, Eldridge, 147

climate change, global, 147

coffee beans on seder plate, 154

Cohen, Israel I., 123–24

Cohen, Tamara, 151

collections of Haggadot, 14–15;
of the author, 2–3; of Stephen Durchslag, 1, 2–4

commentaries: in ArtScroll
Haggadot, 111; in Conservative Haggadah of 1982, 110;
contemporary collections of,

commentaries (*continued*)
83–84; in printed Haggadot,
81–84

communitas, 25

concentration camps: *Ani
Ma'amin* (I Believe) sung in,
131; Haggadah recited from
memory in, 122–24; Hagga-
dah smuggled into, 122;
named in liturgies included
with Haggadot, 135, 137; in
Podwal's image for Wiesel's
Haggadah, 138

Conservative movement,
Haggadot of, 16, 107, 108–10,
132–33, 136

Coppel, Werner, 124–25

copper engraving, 70, 71, 76,
114

Cowan, Lillian, 109

Crimes and Misdemeanors
(film), 171

dance, based on *Echad Mi
Yode'a*, 163–64

"Dayenu": in fairly traditional
Haggadah, 8; referenced in
The Sayer by Lau-Lavie, 160;
in Sheinson's Haggadah for
Holocaust survivors, 129; in
Washington Haggadah, 62;
whacking with scallions
during, 92

Deinard, Ephraim, 65

Deuteronomy: Passover ritual
in, 20, 22; question posed in,

38–39; story of enslavement
and exodus in, 19; wandering
Aramean in, 31–32

digitization: of illuminated
Haggadot, 49; of personalized versions, 154; of Washington Haggadah, 66

Dishon, David, 141

Dropsie Haggadah, 41–42

Durchslag, Stephen, 1, 2–4

Durkheim, Émile, 166

Echad Mi Yode'a (Who Knows
One?), 143, 158–59, 161–62,
163, 179; dance based on,
163–64

Egalitarian Haggadah, 151

Egypt. *See* Exodus story

Einstein, Albert, 97

Eleazar son of Rabbi Zadok,
35, 36

Eliezer ben Elijah Ashkenazi,
64

Elijah Ben Solomon (Vilna
Gaon), 82

Elijah's arrival: in Birds' Head
Haggadah, 52; cup of wine
and, 63–64, 87–88, 135;
heralding the coming of the
Messiah, 52, 63; Miriam's
Cup and, 155; modes of transportation for, 64; in Washington Haggadah, *63*, 63–64;
welcomed in traditional
Haggadah, 8

Elzas, Barnett A., 94

English-language commentaries, in ArtScroll Haggadot, 111

English-language Haggadot: of Arbeter Ring, 106–7; of British Reform movement, 93–94; commissioned by Daniel and Joanna Rose, 144; Guggenheim's unpublished version, 118–19

English translations, 86, 87–88; in Conservative Jewish homes, 109

Epstein, Marc, 48, 52

Eretz Yisrael (Land of Israel): Babylonian Haggadah traditions compared to, 42; Schechter's Haggadah fragments from, 41

eschatological illustrations, 52

Esther, Book of: borrowed images in commentary on, 76–77; Jewish law on hearing of, 11

Ethiopian Jews, 85–86, 187n11

exegetical principles, 46

Exodus, biblical book of: readings from, in British Reform Haggadah of 1842, 93; sources for Passover ritual in, 20–21

Exodus story: biblical injunction to tell the story, 6, 8, 9; foreshadowed in Genesis, 18–19; in Haggadot of Jewish labor movement, 106–7; illustrated in illuminated Haggadot, 50; Israelites crossing the sea in, *115*;

kibbutz Haggadot emphasizing human agency in, 103–4; parent's responsibility to transmit the memory, 38; recalled in *maggid* section of Haggadah, 43, 45; recent oppressive problems compared to, 154; recited from memory in concentration camp, 124; Reconstructionist retelling of, 108, 109; summarized in Deuteronomy, 19

Ezekiel, biblical book of, 168

Ezekiel, Moses, 96

Ezra Synagogue in Old Cairo, 40, 44

Fastag, Azriel-David, 131

Feast of Matzot, in Exodus, 21

Feast of Unleavened Bread, in Leviticus, 21

feminism: Haggadah commentaries with perspective of, 84; New Union Haggadah of 2014 and, 98; students' Haggadot addressing issues of, 161. *See also* women

feminist Haggadot, 149–53; Maxwell House sponsor's distancing from, 75; Miriam's Cup in, 155; Paley's *Seder Masochism*, 140; radical versions replaced by celebration of Jewish women, 151–52; rendering sons as daughters or children, 38 fifth cup of wine: Talmudic debate on, 34–35, 133; as thanksgiving for State of Israel, 133–34

Finkelstein, Louis, 108–9

Foer, Jonathan Safran, 81, 173

food insecurity, 148–49, 154, 158, 172–73

four cups of wine: Abarbanel's commentary on, 83; Alexander's advice on, 87–88; Amsterdam Haggadah's question about, 83; four blessings over, 7, 8, 43, 184n4; reduced to one in British Reform Haggadah, 94; in typical kibbutz Haggadah, 102–3. *See also* wine

four daughters, 38, 151, 152

four questions: Abarbanel's commentary on, 82–83; four Bible verses related to, 38, 183n16; in kibbutz Haggadot, 103; in Mishnah, 29–30; Munich seder in 1946 with no children to ask, 129; in *The Sayer* by Lau-Lavie, 159–60; substitution in Union Haggadah, 95; in traditional Haggadah, 8; traditionally asked by boys, 111

four rabbis, in Birds' Head Haggadah, 50–51

four sons: Abarbanel's commentary on, 83; in Amsterdam Haggadah of 1695, *77*; borrowed images of, in Hakohen's illustrations, 76; as children in retranslated Maxwell house Haggadah, 75; Dropsie Haggadah with no mention of, 41; in kibbutz parody, 100; midrashic influence on, 38–39, 50–51; Reisinger's modern artistic rendering of, 110; replaced by four daughters, 38, 151; in Second Cincinnati Haggadah, *78. See also* four questions; wicked son; wise son

Frank, Anne, 97, 135, 136, 137

freedom: helping others to achieve, 6; Holocaust reference in Reform Haggadah and, 137; hope for more complete liberation and, 173; as Reconstructionist theme, 107–8; referenced in *The Sayer* by Lau-Lavie, 160; Sharansky's memory of Haggadah in Siberia and, 126; symbolized in broken matzah, 88–89, 132; as theme in Haggadah, 6, 8

Freedom Seder, 146–48

Free Zone (film), 165

Friedman, Debbie, 151, 152

Friends of Refugees of Eastern Europe (FREE), 142

Frojmavic, Eva, 55

Gandhi, 147

gender: inclusive language in 2014 New Union Haggadah,

98; retranslated Maxwell house coffee Haggadah and, 74–75; Washington Haggadah and, 62–64; ways of addressing God and, 153

Genesis: illuminated Haggadot with stories from, 52, 54; story of the exodus foreshadowed in, 18–19

genizah, 12, 40

geonim, 40–41

George VI, King of England, 121–22

Gibson, Margaret, 40

Ginsberg, Allen, 147

Gitai, Amos, 165

Glatzer, Nahum N., 141

GLBT Haggadah, seder plates for, 155–56, *157*

Golan Heights Winery Haggadah, 143

Goldberg, Nathan, 109, 141

Greco-Roman symposium: after-dinner revelry of, 27, 39; Jesus's Last Supper and, 28; seder's resemblance to, 7; table ritual of Mishnah and Tosefta and, 27

Greenberg, Yitz, 134

green vegetable, blessing over, 8, 9, 43

Grünberg, Maty, 14, 143, 164

Gubkin, Liora, 133, 136

Guggenheim, Siegfried, 113–19

Gurs Haggadah, 125–26

Haggadah for the Liberated Lamb, 154–55

Haggadah Lepesach of British Reform movement, 93–94

Hakohen, Abraham, 75

Hallel: in Mishnah ceremony, 27, 28; recited over fifth cup of wine, 34

handwashing: Abarbanel's commentary on, 83; in Greco-Roman symposium, 27; in illuminated Haggadot, 51, 55; in steps of seder, 43; in traditional Haggadah, 8

Hanukkah, 13, 72

hares, Haggadah illustrations of, 64–65

Hasidic Haggadot, 16; Lubavitch, 141–42

Hasidic rabbi, in concentration camp, 122–23

Hatikva, 109

Hauptman, Judith, 26

Heschel, Susannah, 145–46

Hezekiah, King, 23

hiddur mitzvah, 48

historiographical Haggadot, 17

history, as source of diverse Haggadot, 17

Hochman, Abraham, 73

Hoffman, Jan, 144

Hoffman, Lawrence, 1, 26

Holbein, Hans, 75

Holocaust: Conservative Haggadah of 1982 with text on, 110; figuring out how to

Holocaust (*continued*)
create postwar Haggadot
and, 132–33; Haggadah
buried in cemetery during,
124; Haggadah written during, 17; Haggadot only in
memory during, 12, 122–24;
Haggadot written from
memory during, 125–26; idea
of all-powerful God and,
170; Israel's day of remembrance for, 104, 189n20; kibbutz Haggadot with early responses to, 113; survivors'
Haggadot, 127–30. *See also*
concentration camps
Holocaust Remembrance Day,
136
Hunger Seder Haggadah,
148–49

illuminated Haggadot, 14;
available facsimiles of four-
teenth-century treasures, 48–
49; Birds' Head Haggadah,
49–54; Christian sources of,
48, 78–79; commissioned by
Daniel and Joanna Rose,
144; commissioned by
wealthy Jewish families, 47–
48; digitized, 49; handwritten in the present day, 66;
iconophobic tendencies possibly interrupting, 47; medieval, 46–49; revived in
seventeenth and eighteenth

centuries, 77–79; Sarajevo
Haggadah, 52, 54–60; standard categories of images in,
50–52; Szyk's Haggadah with
qualities of, 119, *120*; Washington Haggadah, 60–66
Imamovic, Enver, 58
imperfections of Haggadah,
166–70
interfaith families: artichokes as
welcoming symbol for, 154;
Haggadah of Cokie and
Steve Roberts, 117; students
creating Haggadot relevant
to, 161
Iraqi Jews' Haggadot, recovered
in Saddam's basement,
126–27
Israel, State of: Conservative
Haggadah of 1982 with text
on, 110; figuring out recogni-
tion of, in postwar Haggadot, 132; Guggenheim's 1960
Haggadah with prayer for,
118; Jewish labor movement
raising funds for, 106; linked
with Holocaust in postwar
Haggadot, 132–33; national
anthem included in Ameri-
can Conservative Haggadah,
109; national holidays in,
104, 189n20; Orthodox Jews
proposing Haggadah refer-
ences to, 133–34; popular
Haggadot in, 142–43; recent
updates to traditional

Haggadot in, 156–59; Sheinson's conviction of need to
settle in, 129–30; Szyk's
artistic portrayal of pioneers
in, 121
Israel ben Moses, 113
Israel Museum in Jerusalem,
49, 53
Issacher Ber ben Abraham
Eliezer, 71

Jastrow, Morris, 96
Jesus's Last Supper, 28–29
Jewish Labor Bund, 106
Jewish Labor Committee for
Palestine, 106
Jewish labor movement in
America, 105–7
Jewish National Library in Jeru-
salem, 14
Jewish Renewal movement, 147
Jewish soldiers: celebrating
Passover in 1862, 37; in Pales-
tine, 127; in World War II,
127
Jewish Theological Seminary,
108, 128
Joel ben Rabbi Simon, 116
Joel Feibush ben Simeon, 61–
62, 64
Johanan (Talmudic sage), 35–36
Joseph Jacobs Advertising
Agency, 73, 75
Joseph the Demon, 34
Josiah, King, 23
Judah Loew ben Bezalel, 82

Judeo-Italian, 16, 84
Judeo-Spanish (Ladino), 16, 84

Kadima, 150
Kahn, Hermann, 53
Kalderon, Asher, 143
Kalechofsky, Roberta, 154
Kaplan, Mordecai, 108–9
Karaites, 42
Kasher, Menachem, 39, 83,
133–34
Katznelson, 104
Kibbutz Afikim, 100
Kibbutz Ein Harod, 102
kibbutz Haggadot, 90–91, 93,
98–104; early responses to
Holocaust in, 113; as precedent
for innovative seders, 146
Kibbutz Naan, 103
Kibbutz Ramat Yochanan, 100
Kibbutz Tel Yesef, 103
Kibbutz Yagur, 102
King, Martin Luther, Jr., 147
King James Bible of 1611, 79, 79
Klausner, Abraham J., 128
Klawans, Jonathan, 28–29
Klimt, Gustav, 53–54
Klingspor Brothers Press, 114
Ključo, Merima, 60
Koch, Rudolf, 114–15
Kogman-Appel, Katrin, 66
Kohen family, 57
Koppel, Ted, 58
Korech, 43, 135–36. *See also*
sandwich of bitter herbs and
charoset

"Koren Ethiopian Haggada,"
85–86, 187n11
Korkut, Derviš, 57–58
Kredel, Fritz, 115, 118
Kristallnacht, 117
Kulp, Joshua, 183n12
Kushner, Tony, 10

Labendz, Jacob Ari, 17
labor movement, of Jews in
America, 105–7
Labor Zionist Alliance, 105–6
Ladino (Judeo-Spanish), 16, 84
lamb, eaten at seder: Abarbanel's commentary on, 83; replaced in vegetarian Haggadah, 154–55; in Washington
Haggadah, 62. *See also* sacrifice of lambs
Lang, Berel, 130
languages of Haggadot, 16. *See
also* English-language Haggadot; Yiddish
large print Haggadot, 73
Last Supper of Jesus, 28–29
Lau-Lavie, Amichai, 159–60
leader who chants the Haggadah, 11, 33
leaning (reclining), 27, 28, 30,
34, 82, 88, 101
Leib ben Volf, Moshe, 78–79
Leibowitz, Nechama, 83
Leon of Modena, 82, 83
Levi (Talmudic sage), 35–36
Levi, Primo, 135, 137
Leviticus, 20, 21–22

Levy, Richard and Beatrice, 143
Lewis, Agnes, 40
Lilith magazine, 151
Lissitzky, El, 164
Lubavitch Haggadah versions,
141–42
Luria, Isaac Ashkenazi (Ari), 82

maggid section, 35, 43, 45, 134
Maharal of Prague, 82
Maimonides, Moses, 44–46,
131
Malinowski, Bronislaw, 1
Manger, Itik, 164
manna: in Birds' Head Haggadah, 50; evoked in local seder
customs, 92
Mansour, Eli, 141
Marathi, Haggadah written in
Hebrew and, 16, 85
Marks, David Woolf, 93–94
maror, 43, 82, 148. *See also*
bitter herbs
Marum family, 53–54
master of the seder. *See ba'al
haseder*
matzah: Abarbanel's commentary on, 82; Bene Israel Jews
of India and, 85; in Birds'
Head Haggadah, 50; blessing
before eating, 8, 43, 55;
breaking in half, 8, 43, 88,
137; Christian accusations
about, 52; in concentration
camp, 122–23; early decorative motifs for, 47; eaten

with lamb at the Temple, 22; eating retrieved half, 8, 39; in Elie Wiesel's Haggadah, 136; in home ceremony of Tosefta, 26; in illuminated Haggadot, 50, 51; illustrators borrowing images of, 76; in Mishnah version of ceremony, 27, 29; in new practices after destruction of Second Temple, 24; pile of three, 88; precise instructions for, 9; in sandwich of bitter herbs and charoset, 8, 43, 51, 135–36; in Sarajevo Haggadah, 54–55; supermarket Haggadah with coupon for, 5; symbolic meanings of, 30, 55, 88; in Washington Haggadah, 62. *See also* afikomen

matzah snatching, 33–34. *See also* afikomen

Maxwell house coffee Haggadot: Amazon sales of 2019 version, 140, 192n2; author's collection of, 2–3; history of, 73–74; retranslated in English in 2011, 74–75; used by many Conservative Jews, 109; used by many Orthodox Jews, 110–11

Ma'yan, annual women's seders of, 151

medieval illuminated Haggadot, 46–49

Medved, Michael, 145

Menachem, scribe of Birds' Head Haggadah, 50

menorah: outside one's home, 72; Podwal's contrasting illustrations of, 138

Mereimar, 33

Merian, Mattheus, 75

Messer, Tamar, 14

Messiah, 52, 131

messianic ages, 55, 76, 118, 134, 172

Michaelson, Jay, 139

microcalligraphy, 143

Midrash, 24, 37–39; dropped from 1907 Union Haggadah, 95; feminist, 150; four sons and, 38–39, 50–51; symbolic meaning of charoset and, 36

minhag, 92

Miriam's Cup, 98, 152, 155

Mishnah, 24, 27–32; on charoset not commanded by the Torah, 35; Dropsie Haggadah with similarity to, 41–42; engaging with older Passover symbols, 30; on Passover story line, 35; sometimes confirmed by rabbis of the Talmud, 34; Tosefta ceremony compared to, 29

Mishneh Torah of Maimonides, 44

mnemonic for steps of seder, 43

Moriah, Avner, 14, 143

Moses: in Amsterdam Haggadah, 71; in Birds' Head

Moses (*continued*)
Haggadah, 50, 52; as hero of Jewish labor movement, 106; image in 1695 Amsterdam Haggadah, *80*; image in King James Bible, *79*; Maimonides on role of Moses in Haggadah, 44–45; in Sarajevo Haggadah, 54; as social activist in Reconstructionist Haggadah, 108; story of exodus and, 19, 20

Moss, David, 143–44

Mount Sinai, 21, 55

Ms. magazine, 151

musical content: of Guggenheim's unpublished English version, 118; helpful notation for, 96, 116; at Holocaust memorial services, 131; in kibbutz Passover observance, 102; at Ma'yan's annual women's seders, 151; in pilgrimage holiday at Temple, 22; in Union Haggadah, 96. *See also* songs

My People's Passover Haggadah, 83–84

Naharin, Ohad, 163

Nathan ben Rabbi Salomo, 116

Natronai, Rabbi defending Babylonian Haggadah, 42

Nazis: attempted theft of Sarajevo Haggadah, 57; depicted in Sheinson's Haggadah, 128;

Guggenheim's flight from, 117–18; style labeled degenerate art by, 115; Syzk's artwork alerting world to threat of, 119, 121; Zuckerman's trust in God to determine fate of, 126

Neue Sachlichkeit (new objectivity), 115

New Haggadah of Mordecai Kaplan, 108–9

"Next year in Jerusalem": in Birds' Head Haggadah, 53; in Guggenheim's Haggadot, 116–17, 118; omitted by Cookie and Steve Roberts, 117; removed from Union Haggadah, 95; restored in New Union Haggadah, 97–98; in twentieth-century variations on Haggadah, 93

A Night to Remember: A Haggadah of Contemporary Voices, 137

Nimrod, Naomi, 151, 152

"Notes on Akiba" (Kushner), 10

Numbers, biblical book of, 22

Nuremberg Mahzor, 49

Obama, Barack, 74

Offenbach Haggadah, 113–19; edition of 1722, 113–14; Israelites crossing the sea in, *115*

Off Our Backs, 150

Oppenheim, Moritz, 96

Oppenheimer banking family, Haggadah of, 13–14

oral tradition, 11–12; of Passover ritual after destruction of the Temple, 26; practices preserved as, 92; still dominant in eleventh century, 42–43

orange on seder plate, *157*; as feminist innovation, 98, 145–46, 152; in GLBT Haggadah, 155, 156; representing Judaism that welcomes diversity, 146

Oren, Rony, 143

Orthodox Judaism, 16, 107, 110–12; liberal adherents of, 134, 148; resistance to Holocaust references in Haggadot, 133. *See also* Hasidic Haggadot

pairs, danger of, 34–35

Paley, Grace, 151

Paley, Nina, 140

paper cutting, 143

Papo, Mira, 57–58

Parisian Haggadah of 1869, 88

parodies of Haggadot, 99–100

Passover Haggadah: The Feast of Freedom, 110

Passover in Egypt, 20

Passover of the Generations, 21

Passover pilgrimage to the Temple, 22–23; destruction of Temple and, 24–26; as powerful group religious experience, 25, 166–67. *See also* sacrifice of lambs

pedagogical imperfections of Haggadah, 167–68

People of the Book (Brooks), 59–60

Podwal, Mark, 14, 138

Pogrebin, Letty Cottin, 151

Portman, Natalie, 165

potato chip on seder plate, 154

Prague Haggadah of 1526, 88

printed Haggadot, 67–89; borrowed images in, 75–81; commentaries in, 81–84; emerging despite destruction of presses, 69; explanations in, 86–89, 116; first known example of, 69; influence of Amsterdam Haggadah of 1695, 69–70; promotional materials in, 70–75; rabbis invited to introduce specific versions, 69; rapidly increasing number of versions, 68; significant early examples of, 67; songs included in, 161–65; of translations, 84–86, 87–88. *See also* Amsterdam Haggadah of 1695

promotional materials, 70–75

Provencali family, 65

Psalms: Hallel selection of, 27, 28, 34; in home ceremony of Mishnah, 27, 42; in home ceremony of Tosefta, 26; in Passover at Temple in Jerusalem, 22; recited from memory by Sharansky in Siberia,

Psalms (*continued*)
126; in traditional Haggadah,
8, 9; vengeance as theme in,
64, 186n22
Purim, 76

Rabban Gamaliel the Younger,
30, 42
Rabinowicz, Rachel Anne, 110
Rav Sheshet, 33
Rav Yosef, 33
reclining. *See* leaning
(reclining)
Reconstructionist Judaism, 16,
107–9
Reform Haggadot, 16, 90–91,
92–98; of 2012 with attention to Holocaust, 137–38;
British, 93–94; Union
Haggadah versions, 94–98
Reform Jews, holding one seder
on first night, 187n1
refugees: Israeli Haggadot
bringing awareness to, 156–
57; students creating Haggadot to address, 161; Trump
administration and, 157–58
Regelson, Abraham, 111
Reisinger, Dan, 110
Religious Liberty (sculpture by
Moses Ezekiel), 96
The Republican Haggadah,
158–59
revenge (vengeance): New
Union Haggadah of 1974
and, 97; Szyk's belief in, 121;

text expressing a wish for,
7–8, 64; as theme in psalms,
64, 186n22; Zuckerman's
trust in God to decide on, 126
Rice Paper Haggadah, 149–50
Roberts, Cokie and Steve, 117
Rose, Daniel and Joanna S., 144
Roth, Cecil, 47
Rothstein, Edward, 15–16
Rubiner, Michael, 140
Russian Haggadot, 142; in
women's seders, 193n16
Russian Social Democratic
Workers' Party, 106

Saadya Gaon, 40, 42
Sacks, Jonathan, 83, 88–89
sacrifice of lambs: on departure
from Egypt, 20; made sym-
bolic with food and drink, 7;
pilgrimage to the Temple
and, 7, 22–23, 24, 166, 172;
replacing Abraham's son
Isaac, 19; as symbol in Mishnah Passover ceremony, 30.
See also lamb, eaten at seder
Salter, James, 4
Samuel ben Solomon, 43
sandwich of bitter herbs and
charoset, 8, 43, 51, 135–36
Sarajevo Haggadah, 52, 54–60;
creative works based on, 59–
60; dramatic life of, 56–60;
image of dark-skinned
woman in, 55–56, 59
The Sayer by Lau-Lavie, 159–60

Schechter, Solomon, 40–41, 44

Schechter Haggadah, 17

Schocken's 1979 *Passover Haggadah*, 141

Schoenberg, E. Randol, 53

Schwesig, Karl, 125

Second Cincinnati Haggadah, *78*, 78–79

second commandment, 50

secular kibbutz Haggadah, 102–3

secular third seders, 91, 93, 105–7, 146

secular Yiddish *hagodes*, 90–91, 93

seder: additions if falls on a Saturday night, 64–65; collapsing of time in, 21; distinctive regional customs of, 91–92; Jesus's Last Supper and, 28–29; meaning "order," 7; publicizing miracle of God's rescue, 72; slavery and freedom as theme in, 6, 8; steps to be followed, 8, 43–44

Seder Eve (Oppenheim painting), 96

The Seder Masochism: A Haggadah and Anti-Haggadah, 140

seder plate: created in sixteenth century, 43; new Haggadot with unusual objects for, 154–56, *157*; orange on, 98, 145–46, 152, 155, 156, *157*

Sephardic Haggadot, 16; Ethiopian Jews encouraged to conform to, 85–86; with images of stories from Genesis, 52; popular today, 141; Sarajevo Haggadah, 52, 54–60

Sephardic Jews: English translation for, 87; exiled from Spain in 1492, 69, 169–70; Haggadot with Ladino instructions for, 84–85; of Iberian peninsula, 44; owning a Haggadah by fourteenth century, 46

September 11th Memorial Museum, 25

Serotta, Edward, 58–59

Shahn, Ben, 14, 164

Shalit, Gilad, 156, 172

Sharansky, Natan, 126

Sharet, Yehuda, 102

Sheinson, Yosef Dov, 127–30

Sheriff-Alperin, Jacob, 158–59

Shlonsky, Abraham, 135, 136

Sidi, Eliyahu, 14, 143

Silber, David, 83

Silverman, Morris, 109

Sinatra, Frank, 106

Six-Day War of 1967, Haggadot issued after, 17

sober seder, 155

social issues, seders addressing, 144–49. *See also* feminism

socialist activists of Jewish labor movement, 105–7

socialist parodies of Haggadah, 99, 188n12

sofer, 12

Soloveitchik, Joseph, 83
Soncino family of Guadalajara, Spain, 69
Soncino Press in Italy, 81
Song of Songs: in kibbutz Haggadah, 102; recited at seder's end, 73
songs: Babylonian Haggadah expanded with, 44; in Holocaust Haggadah written from memory, 125; included in print Haggadot, 161–65; popular liturgical songs, 8, 9; role in keeping the Haggadah alive, 171. *See also* musical content
Soviet persecution of Jews, 126, 142, 145, 172
Spitzer, Juliet I., 164
Steinem, Gloria, 151
Stella, Frank, 164
Stern, David, 21, 66
Strassfeld, Michael, 110
supermarket Haggadot, 2–3, 5. *See also* Maxwell house coffee Haggadot
Sutton, David, 141
Syzk, Arthur, 14, 119
Szyk Haggadah, 119–22, *120*, 171

Talmud, 24, 32–37; on angels rejoicing as Egyptians drown, 97; categories of rules debated by, 35; debate on charoset, 35–37; debate on number of cups of wine, 34–35, 133; debate on

Passover story line, 35; printed with text surrounded by commentary, 81
tangerines, 146, 154
Tarfon (Talmudic sage), 34
technology: future uses for Haggadot, 172–73. *See also* digitization
Temples in Jerusalem: day of mourning marking the destruction of, 133; destruction of Second Temple, 7, 24, 26; dream of rebuilding, 172; images in Sarajevo Haggadah, 54; Passover pilgrimage to, 7, 22–23, 166–67; priestly classes of, 88; Shavuot pilgrimage of Israelite farmers, 7, 31. *See also* sacrifice of lambs
ten plagues: in Birds' Head Haggadah, 50; missing from Reconstructionist Haggadah, 108; reframed as ecological disasters, 147–48; repurposed for Jewish labor movement, 107; tenth plague killing Egyptian children, 20, 76; today's examples of, suggested by HIAS, 157–58; in traditional Haggadah, 8, 10; Union Haggadah and, 95, 97
theological imperfections of Haggadah, 168–70
third seders, 91, 93, 105–7, 146
Thomas S., 124

Thoreau, Henry, 147
Tisha B'Av (Ninth of Av), 133
tomato on seder plate, 154
Torah: books included in, 180,
    182n1; burned by German
    Army, 57; charoset as mitz-
    vah and, 35–36; four children
    with questions and, 38; most
    sacred commandments in, 35;
    museum ethics in dealing
    with scrolls of, 190n12; in
    open ark in Sarajevo Hagga-
    dah, 55; rules governing pro-
    duction and usage of, 11, 12–
    13; table ritual of Mishnah
    and, 27
Tosefta, 24, 26–27, 29
Touster, Saul, 128–29
translations, 84–86; into
    English, 86, 87–88, 109; into
    German, 116; sometimes
    badly done, 86
transliterations of Hebrew: in
    ArtScroll Haggadot, 112; in
    Maxwell House Haggadah,
    75; in Offenbach Haggadah,
    116
Trump administration, 157–59
Tsint on di likht, in third seder,
    107
Turner, Edith, 25
Turner, Victor, 25
Tzli Esh, 83

Union Haggadah of Reform
    movement, 94–98

unleavened bread, 20, 21. See
    also matzah
Uri L'Tzedek, 148

vegetarian Haggadah, 154–55
The Velveteen Rabbi's Haggadah
    for Pesach, 153
Venetian Haggadot, 67, 75; of
    1609, 84; of 1629, 2, 83
vengeance. See revenge
    (vengeance)
Vilna Gaon (Elijah Ben
    Solomon), 82
Vistorini, Giovanni
    Domenico, 56

Walzer, Michael, 27
wandering Aramean, 31
Washington Haggadah, 60–66;
    Harvard University Press fac-
    simile edition, 65–66; hu-
    morous spirit of, 61–65; illus-
    trated with Elijah on a
    donkey, 63; Library of Con-
    gress digitization of, 66;
    Library of Congress facsimile
    edition, 65; scribe and illumi-
    nator of, 61–62
Waskow, Arthur, 146–48
When Do We Eat (film), 171
wicked daughter, in feminist
    Haggadah, 152
wicked son, 76, 82; in kibbutz
    parody, 100
Wiener, Shmuel, 15
Wiesel, Elie, 97, 135–36, 138

Wiesel, Moses, 71

wine: fifth cup of, 34–35, 133–34; in Greco-Roman symposium, 27; in illuminated Haggadot, 51; at Jesus's Last Supper, 7; in Mishnah version of ceremony, 27; Talmudic debate about, 34–35, 133; in Tosefta version of ceremony, 26; in Washington Haggadah, 62. *See also* four cups of wine

Wise, Yaakov, 14

wise son, 38–39, 76, 83; as computer geek, 143

Wolff, Barbara, 14, 144

Woman in Gold (film), 53

women: as editors of Haggadot, 110; Passover commentaries by, 83–84; seders at Yale University for, 83. *See also* feminism

woodcuts, 68, 69, 114, *115*, 128

Yaari, Abraham, 15

Yemen, 44, 156

Yerushalmi, Yosef Hayim, 15, 171

Yiddish: Haggadot including translation into, 84; Haggadot printed in, 73; of immigrants to North America, 105–6; of Sheinson's Haggadah for Holocaust survivors, 127–28; socialist parodies of Haggadah in, 188n12; socialist parodies of Haggadah written in, 99; spoken by immigrants to America, 91

Yiddish stage, 106

Yudlov, Yitzhak, 15

Zangwill, Israel, 86

Zeta-Jones, Catherine, 60

Zevach Pesach (Passover Sacrifice), 82–83, 169–70

Zion, Mishael, 137, 141

Zion, Noam, 137, 141

Zionism: Haggadot focused on establishing a Jewish homeland and, 172; Haggadot for Holocaust survivors and, 128; *Hatikva* as anthem of First Zionist Congress, 109; Labor Zionist Alliance, 105–6; range of stances toward, 93; Szyk's promotion of, 121, 122

Zuckerman, Aryeh Ludwig, 125, 126

Zweig, Stefan, 118